Case Studies in Corrections

Case Studies in Corrections

Examples, Exercises, Discussion Points, and Practitioner Interviews

Barbara Peat
INDIANA UNIVERSITY NORTHWEST

CAROLINA ACADEMIC PRESS

Durham, North Carolina

Library of Congress Cataloging-in-Publication Data

Peat, Barbara.
  Case studies in corrections : examples, exercises, discussion
points, and practitioner interviews / Barbara Peat.
      p. cm.
  ISBN 978-1-59460-823-0 (alk. paper)
  1. Corrections--Administration. 2. Correctional institutions--
Administration. I. Title.

  HV8756.P43 2011
  365.068--dc22

                    2010045793

CAROLINA ACADEMIC PRESS
700 Kent Street
Durham, North Carolina 27701
Telephone (919) 489-7486
Fax (919) 493-5668
www.cap-press.com

Printed in the United States of America
2017 Printing

This book is dedicated to my beloved parents,
who believed in my abilities,
supported my interests, and
shared in the love and care of my children.

Contents

Preface   xi

Chapter One · Introduction   3
   Assignment 1.1   5

Chapter Two · Institutional Corrections   7
  Introduction   7
  Case Studies   8
   Prison — Henry   8
   Assignment 2.1   10
   Jail — Vince   10
   Assignment 2.2   13
   Halfway House — Pete   14
   Assignment 2.3   16
   Work Release — Ralph   17
   Assignment 2.4   20
   Residential Mental Health Placement — Linda   21
   Assignment 2.5   23
   Residential Substance Abuse Program — Jacob   24
   Assignment 2.6   26

Chapter Three · Community Corrections   29
  Introduction   29
  Case Studies   30
   Probation — Bill   30
   Assignment 3.1   31
   Parole — Brian   32
   Assignment 3.2   34

Electronic Monitoring — Doug 34
Assignment 3.3 37
Day Treatment Program — Frank 37
Assignment 3.4 40
House Arrest — Cindy 41
Assignment 3.5 43
County Drug Court Program — Phil 44
Assignment 3.6 46

Chapter Four • Juvenile Intervention Services 47
Introduction 47
Case Studies 47
First Offender Program — Scott 47
Assignment 4.1 49
Family Intervention Program — The Green Family 50
Assignment 4.2 52
Substance Abuse Program — Kenny 53
Assignment 4.3 55
Juvenile Detention Facility — Holly 56
Assignment 4.4 58
Correctional Placement — Gary 59
Assignment 4.5 61
Aftercare Services — Marti 61
Assignment 4.6 63

Chapter Five • Correctional Administration 65
Introduction 65
Case Studies 65
Budgetary Constraints 65
Assignment 5.1 67
Adjusting Caseloads 68
Assignment 5.2 71
Provision of Inmate Programs 72
Assignment 5.3 75
Personnel Issues 76
Assignment 5.4 78

Legal Issues	79
Assignment 5.5	81
Accreditation	82
Assignment 5.6	83

Chapter Six • Reports 85
Introduction	85
Presentence Report	85
Example Presentence Report	86
Assignment 6.1	91
Probation Violation Report	91
Example Probation Violation Report	94
Assignment 6.2	95
Alternative Probation Violation Report	96
Assignment 6.3	97
Parole Violation Reports	99
Example Parole Violation Report	100
Assignment 6.4	102
Case Notes	102
Example Case Notes — John Doe	104
Assignment 6.5	110
Parole Plan	110
Example Parole Plan	112
Assignment 6.6	112
Community Corrections Programs	113
Example Community Corrections Program Referral	114
Assignment 6.7	116

Chapter Seven • Integrating Case Studies with Career Development 117
Introduction	117
Exploring Options	118
Job Shadowing	119
Completing Internships	120
Volunteer	123
Utilize Campus Career Services	123
Attend Job Fairs	124

Engaging in Reflection 126
Developing a Degree Plan 127
Increasing Marketability 129
Searching for Employment 131
Preparing for the Selection Process 133
Summary 135
   Assignment 7.1 135

Chapter Eight • Practitioner Interviews 137
Interviews 137
   The Questionnaire 138
Participant Invitation 139
Employment Positions of Respondents and Length
   of Employment 140
Responses to General Questions 140
Summary of Key Points 156
Closing Comments 157

Index 159

Preface

The primary purpose of this book is to offer supplemental material to assist in understanding basic content information on a variety of correctional topics including institutional and community corrections, adult and juvenile offender risks and needs, and administrative and management principles. Case studies, example reports, practitioner interviews, and an informational guide for career development are among the tools used to focus on the stated purpose.

Learning tools in the form of questions, discussion topics, and assignments are included at the end of each case study. The versatility of the potential use of these tools is a significant strength of this book. The way these tools can be used and their prospective value are at the discretion of the instructor. They can be used to evaluate the students' application of content learning, such as knowledge of terminology and understanding of definitions, familiarity with criminal justice topics, and awareness of current events. The tools are also an excellent means to assess students' critical thinking and other higher order learning abilities such as synthesis, integration, and comparing and contrasting. Some of the exercises require students to demonstrate their research skills. Many of the questions require students to provide a rationale or justification for an answer, encouraging students to state their opinions and support their ideas using integration of knowledge learned in other courses, content specific information, and additional readings and research such as information in government data bases. Some of the questions and topics can foster discussions of ethical issues and create venues for students to reflect on personal biases. All of the tools have the potential to increase the depth and breadth of learning along with awareness of social issues and local and national current events.

The learning tools included after each case can be used in multiple formats. For example, instructors can assign them as individual out-of-class homework, out-of-class group assignments, and in-class individual and group activities, as well as in-class debates, in or out-of-class research, and quiz or test questions.

The case studies and the learning tools provide an opportunity for students to become acquainted with correctional operations and interaction of the three basic components of the criminal justice system—policing, courts, and corrections. Although the case studies are fictional and were developed specifically for students to demonstrate their level of knowledge and skill development, the issues presented strike a chord of reality. The cases used in combination with the information gathered through the practitioner interviews and the career development guide provide students with a learning experience they do not routinely get from traditional classroom lecture styles used in many courses.

An additional benefit of the arrangement of the content of this book is its alignment with many introductory corrections texts. These texts commonly provide information about prisons and jails, probation and parole, alternative interventions such as drug and mental health courts, juvenile services, intermediate sanctions like work release and house arrest, and administration and management of correctional operations. Chapter Two on institutional corrections includes cases depicting a violent offender with prison adjustment problems, a young property offender with mental health issues incarcerated in the county jail, a drug offender residing in a half-way house program, an older violent offender with an extensive criminal background residing in a work release program after serving a lengthy prison sentence, a female offender residing in a county mental health facility, and a young male offender residing in a residential substance abuse treatment facility. Chapter Three on community corrections includes cases of an offender sentenced to probation for property and drug offenses, an offender serving prison time for a violent offense returning to the community on parole, an offender serving prison time for a sex offense returning to the community on parole, a young man with mental health challenges convicted of property offenses attending a day treatment program, a young female offender convicted of drug crimes serving probation time under house arrest, and a young male offender sentenced to a drug court program. Chapter Four on juveniles and corrections includes cases involving various intervention services including a first offender program, family intervention services, a substance abuse program, detention facility placement, correction department facility placement, and aftercare services. Chapter Five on administration and management in corrections includes scenarios exploring a variety of topics focusing on budgetary constraints, adjusting caseloads, provision of inmate programs, human resources management, litigation, and accreditation.

Instructors can assign readings from the main text and use the cases from these four chapters to increase the depth and breadth of the students' understanding of applying book information to real life. The example reports commonly used in correctional operations, included in Chapter Six, provide even more opportunities for the instructor to integrate content with experiential learning. In combination, Chapter Seven and Chapter Eight provide information students can use to make decisions about careers in corrections, including factors to keep in mind when deciding if a career in corrections is a good fit.

Instructors can use this book in advanced courses in addition to introduction to corrections classes. The material is suitable for use in a course focused on career exploration. The higher order thinking skills required for many of the case study questions and assignments make it a good choice for upper division courses in correctional administration and management, juvenile delinquency, offender re-entry, and alternative sanctions, to name but a few. Instructors in related disciplines such as social work, sociology, and psychology may also find the book appropriate as a supplemental text.

Case Studies in Corrections

Chapter One

Introduction

Readers will learn or have already learned that there are many facets to the study of corrections. Although many associate corrections solely with incarceration in prisons and jails, this field not only spans institutional placement but also includes community interventions and numerous alternative sanctions for both juvenile and adult offenders. These sentencing options are provided through the public sector and not-for-profit and for-profit organizations. The availability and variety of sentencing options often depends on the county and state in which the offender resides.

The purpose of this book is to provide the reader with a broad based learning experience through the use of fictional case studies, examples of reports commonly used in corrections, questionnaire responses from practitioners, and career-related information. In combination, the material covered can assist students in gaining a better understanding of correctional employment.

To gain the greatest benefit from this book it is important that the reader use the learning tools included at the ends of the chapters to construct individual opinions and demonstrate an understanding of critical points dealing with specific correctional topics. Although the instructor may select only a few of the learning tool options available, readers may consider independently responding to other questions and activities not required for the class. Through such self-development the reader can better understand the content or, at the very least and perhaps equally important, become a better informed citizen. The activities at the end of this chapter are a good starting point to develop the type of reflection and critical thinking that is needed for future activities covered in succeeding chapters.

Chapters Two through Five are centered on numerous fictional case studies. Although these case studies cover a wide span of issues correctional personnel and offenders routinely encounter, they by no means include everything that can occur in corrections. The variability of services, sentencing alternatives, and individual case information is part of what makes corrections such an interesting field to study and a dynamic career option. The cases are developed both to pique the interest of the reader and to provide opportunities for numerous and varied learning experiences through the activities included after each case.

The material in Chapter Six focuses on some of the basic reports used in correctional work. Examples and case studies provide an opportunity for readers to understand common elements and uses of reports. The learning tools at the end of the chapter should facilitate the readers' integration of content learning with personal opinion.

Chapter Seven focuses on a variety of suggestions that can assist readers in exploring career options in corrections. Some of the information pertains specifically to determining if any of the multitudes of career options would be personally suitable. The next part of the chapter provides tips for increasing employment opportunities by improving marketability and information about how to search for employment and how to prepare for the selection process.

The last chapter of the book provides the reader with insight into what work in corrections is really like, based on questionnaire responses provided by practitioners in a variety of correctional positions. Those who work in the system are in the best position to provide valuable information that can assist in making decisions as to whether or not to pursue correctional work as a career.

In combination, the material in this book provides a variety of learning experiences. The value of the book content, in general, and the learning tools, in particular, depends heavily on the motivation of the reader. The benefits to be reaped will be influenced by the amount of time, reflection, critical thinking, and, where appropriate, research engaged in on the journey to learning more about the interesting and dynamic field of corrections. Now, let's get started with some activities to prepare for an interactive learning experience.

Assignment 1.1

1. Without looking through a corrections textbook or doing any additional research on the subject, create a list of every sanction (sentencing option) that you can think of. Just include the terms; you don't need to describe them or define them.

2. Create a line chart (can be hand drawn) that categorizes the sanctions you listed in #1 from what would be considered least punitive to most punitive. In preparing this graphic you may consider grouping some of the sanctions by category.

3. Using the list you created in #1, state which sanction you think is used the most frequently with offenders today (nationally). What do you think is used the least?

4. Which of the sanctions of those you listed in your response to #1 do you think is the most costly; which is the least costly?

5. Which of the sanctions of those you listed in your response to #1 (other than the death penalty) do think would deter offenders from recidivating? Explain your reasoning for your response.

6. How many people in the nation do you think are under any type of correctional supervision in the nation today? Of this number, how many do you think are incarcerated in a correctional facility (prison)?

7. Create two lists of correctional services, one list based on institutional corrections and one list based on community corrections.

8. Based on the lists you created in response to exercise #7, identify all positions or job titles of those involved in providing the services. Again, make two separate lists, one for institutional correctional services (such as superintendent, correctional officer, etc.) and one for community correctional services (such as probation officer, substance abuse counselor, etc.).

9. If you had to choose, which job position would you pursue for employment in corrections? Explain your answer providing information about why you think you would like this career choice and why you would be well-suited for such a position.

Chapter Two

Institutional Corrections

Introduction

This chapter focuses on a variety of issues that correctional employees may encounter in providing services to the incarcerated adult offender. After each case study a list of questions is provided to serve as discussion points, homework assignments, topics for individual or group in or out-of-class activities, and quiz and/or test subject matter. The questions should encourage the readers to reflect on the issues presented in the facts of each case. The reader is encouraged to thoroughly consider the issues presented and apply information learned in courses, knowledge of the criminal justice system (such as through employment and awareness of current events), review of research, and personal awareness, where appropriate. Each incarcerated adult offender has his/her own individual circumstances and life situation, as well as personality traits, adaptation abilities, and behavioral patterns. This chapter focuses on six very different cases: (1) a violent offender with prison adjustment problems, (2) a young property offender with mental health issues who is incarcerated in the county jail, (3) a drug offender residing in a half-way house, (4) an older violent offender with an extensive criminal background who is in a work release program after serving a lengthy prison sentence, (5) a female offender residing in a county mental health facility, and (6) a young male offender residing in a residential substance abuse treatment facility.

Case Studies

Prison — Henry

Henry is a 32-year-old male who has been housed in a medium security prison for the past three years of a 12 year sentence on a conviction for second degree murder. Based on the state's good time policy, Henry has a projected release date in three years. He will have served half of his original sentence. The sentence resulted from a plea agreement.

The presentencing report indicates that the second degree murder charge stemmed from Henry's involvement in a robbery of a convenience store. During the robbery Henry's co-defendant shot the clerk who later died of a gunshot wound to the head after having been in a coma for 16 days. Henry was originally charged with first degree murder, but as a result of the plea agreement, the charge was reduced to second degree. Henry testified at the co-defendant's trial, implicating him as the one who shot the clerk. The state's evidence verified his testimony.

Henry has spent the majority of his adult life under correctional supervision, first having served three years' probation on a burglary conviction, next nine months in jail followed by two years on probation for possession of cocaine, followed by two years in prison with a subsequent 12 months on parole on a robbery conviction. He has not completed any of his probationary or parole terms due to subsequent arrests and/or failure to comply with technical conditions such as reporting as required, gaining and maintaining employment, and not associating with other known felons.

During the past three years in prison, Henry has had seven disciplinary actions stemming from fights with other inmates, the consequence being spending time in disciplinary segregation. He has had six disciplinary actions for failure to comply with work requirements and three disciplinary actions resulting from possession of contraband, all involving possession of tobacco products. The consequence for these non-violent infractions resulted in removal of privileges. The latest report filed by the cell-block counselor notes, "Henry has made a poor adjustment to prison life and there are no indications that the consequences received have led to positive changes." Henry has not had any visitors since being incarcerated, nor does he receive any communication from family members or others. He has occasionally attended non-denominational worship services. The only staff member Henry has expressed any favorable response to is the Chaplain. Henry does not attend any counseling or job training sessions. His assigned work detail has been predominately in the cafeteria, not in food preparation but with clean-up crews. Henry does not express interest in any hobby. He does not check out any reading materials from the prison library and does not have any reading material in his cell.

Henry dropped out of high school at the beginning of the ninth grade. He has not participated in education programs at the prison, nor has he shown any inclination to do so in the future. Information in the presentencing report indicates that Henry was held back three times during elementary years due to poor grades and lack of progress in learning. Henry has never held a job. He is single with two children, ages seven and four, from prior relationships with two different women to whom he was not married. No child support has been ordered.

Jim, a newly employed case manager with the corrections department, has been assigned as Henry's case manager. Jim has been instructed by his supervisor to review Henry's file, complete an updated risk and needs assessment, and develop a case management plan that includes detailed goals for Henry over the next three years. The supervisor has also asked Jim to determine if Henry should continue serving time in the medium security prison or be transferred either to maximum or minimum restrict security. Jim should determine if there is any need for a psychological evaluation. Due to budgetary restrictions, psychological evaluations are requested only when the case manager indicates the evaluation could produce information critical to the appropriate development of services with a high potential for reducing recidivism.

Assignment 2.1

1. Provide a list of what you consider "risks" in this case in regard to satisfactory adjustment to incarceration. Focus on the "cause" of risk (such as failure to participate in counseling sessions), not the evidence of risk (such as number of disciplinary actions).

2. Provide a list of what you consider "needs" in this case. Be specific and provide justification for the need(s) by citing specifics based on the information presented.

3. Based on the identified risks and needs, develop a case management plan for Henry that includes goals and a timeline reasonable to expect achievement within the ensuing three years Henry will be in prison.

4. How would you rate the likelihood that Henry will successfully complete the two-year mandatory parole period upon release from prison? Explain your reasoning. What do you think are the greatest impediments to successful completion?

5. Do you think that Jim should recommend that Henry be transferred to maximum security? If yes, do you recommend he be housed in maximum security for the remainder of his sentence? Explain your answer. If no, do you recommend that he continue to be housed at the medium security facility or be transferred to minimum security? Be sure to provide a rationale for your answer, and discuss length of time to be served and where.

6. If Jim recommends that a psychological evaluation be completed, what is the justification for the recommendation? Be sure to be specific in citing information from Henry's case.

7. If Jim were to focus on one positive aspect of Henry's interactions since being incarcerated, what would that be? How could this interaction be used to encourage positive change?

Jail—Vince

Vince is a 24-year-old male who is currently being housed in the county jail for 90 days prior to release on probation for three years on a burglary conviction. The criminal justice system is familiar with Vince, as he has been in and out of jail, residential placement, day treatment programs, and psychiatric hospital units over the past several years. The recent burglary conviction, is the most serious felony for which he has been convicted. His prior offenses include misdemeanor criminal trespass (four separate arrests), breaking and entering (two separate arrests), and vandalism (five separate arrests). Vince has been diagnosed with paranoid schizophrenic disorder. His IQ score of 83 also indicates a possible mild intellectual disability. His record reflects one prior probationary term, for which he received an unsatisfactory discharge as the result of failure to report as required by the probation officer and an arrest for criminal trespass.

The records reflect that Vince was frequently tardy and truant during the time he was enrolled in the public school system from the time he started in the local schools at the beginning of the fourth grade. The presenting report indicates that no records were obtained for school performance prior to that time period since Vince's family moved to the community where he currently resides when Vince was 10. After an academic evaluation, the public school system determined that Vince required individualized instruction in a socially controlled setting. He was placed in an alternative high school due to his developmental challenges and personality disorder. Vince attended an alternative high school but dropped out at the beginning of the eleventh grade.

Vince resides with his mother and maternal grandmother, never having lived away from home. Upon dropping out of the eleventh grade at the age of 19 (he was held back to repeat the sixth grade) his mother sought Social Security benefits to subsidize his living expenses. The presentence report indicates that both the mother and grandmother appear to be strongly supportive of Vince and sincerely committed to working with community resources to assist Vince in attending a variety of assistance programs. However, they frequently encounter two major challenges in providing supervision: (1) Vince frequently self-withdraws from prescribed medications for the personality disorder, and (2) Vince adamantly defends his choice to leave the residence and the assistance programs whenever he chooses. On the occasions when Vince has been hospitalized to get started back on the prescribed medications, his behavior has become more stabilized, his attendance at various programs more regular, and his compliance with expectations from his mother and grandmother improved. Unfortunately, periods of stability are becoming more infrequent.

A review of the police reports regarding Vince's prior arrests presents a pattern: Vince enters residences and vacant buildings, such as storage sheds and garages, where he has no legal right to be. If a property has been left unsecured, Vince just simply enters. If Vince decides that he wants to enter a secured building, Vince has at times broken windows or kicked open doors to gain entrance. Vince and his family reside in a very small community. The residents are aware of the challenges Vince's family face in managing his behavior and have tried to be understanding of the situation. On a positive note, when told to leave a location where he is not supposed to be, Vince has complied without incident. On a couple of occasions, however, a resident has lodged a complaint with Vince's mother because of destruction of property. Damages have been repaired and/or reimbursed by Vince's maternal uncle. Although records indicate that residents have witnessed bizarre behavior and overt verbal confusion, Vince has never been threatening or physically aggressive to anyone.

The detention officers of the county jail have contacted the sentencing judge to complain about Vince's behavior in jail. His medications are closely monitored and there are no overt indications that he is experiencing hallucinations or is delusional. However, his failure to comply with jail regulations and his apparent lack of understanding what is expected of him in regards to interactions with detention officers, staff, and other detainees have presented issues in managing his movements within the jail. He has been verbally aggressive toward staff when told to leave his cell for counseling sessions, mealtime, or recreation. The jail classification officer had placed Vince in his own cell and has recommended that he not be in close proximity to any other jail detainees for fear that Vince may be victimized. The jail superintendent has requested that the judge amend the sentence to allow Vince to begin his probationary period immediately.

After the closing several decades ago of many of the nation's residential mental health facilities, individuals experiencing similar challenges as Vince were expected to reside with relatives or assume independent or semi-independent living. Because of the closings the percentage of individuals with mental health disorders who come to the attention of the criminal justice system increased dramatically.

In Vince's case, the judge does not have an available sentencing option for long-term residential care. She has contacted the county probation department to discuss possible arrangements for early release of Vince from the jail. She has also requested that the jail provide her with a case management plan for Vince if he is to remain in custody.

Assignment 2.2

1. Do you think that the sentence given to Vince was appropriate? Why or why not? Be detailed in explaining your rationale for your position. If you say "no," what do you think should have been the sentence given to Vince? Explain your answer.

2. Do you think that the jail classification officer made the appropriate placement for Vince in the jail? Why or why not? Provide detail in the rationale for your position on this decision.

3. What should be included in the jail's case management plan for the remainder of time Vince must serve on the 90-day jail sentence? Be sure to include in the case management plan a detailed daily schedule for Vince, including how much time he is to be in his cell each day, what jail programs he may attend, the type of recreation appropriate for his circumstances, etc.

4. What outside agencies would you involve in providing services for Vince? Explain your reasoning for their inclusion. Be sure to include in your explanation the expected goals for their involvement.

5. If you were assigned to be Vince's probation officer, what would you include in the case management plan? Be sure to be detailed in what you would require of Vince while on probation.

6. Do you think that Vince would be a good candidate for electronic monitoring? Why or why not?

7. On a scale of 1 to 10, with 10 being the highest probability for success and 1 being the highest chance for failure, how would you rate Vince's abilities to successfully complete his three-year probationary period? Explain your reasoning.

8. What is the name of the policy/action that resulted in closing many mental health hospitals during the 1970s? What were the reasons given for the closures? Do you think that this was an appropriate course of action? Why or why not? What have been the positive and negative outcomes of the closings?

9. Vince's situation is not unusual. Many people under correctional supervision, whether it be in jail or prison or in community placement (probation or parole) have a diagnosed mental illness and/or developmental disorder. What do you think is the appropriate involvement of the criminal justice system in these cases? Be detailed in your response, suggesting alternatives and your reasoning for those suggestions.

Halfway House — Pete

Pete is a 37-year-old male who is currently serving 12 months in a halfway house as a result of a conviction for possession of drug paraphernalia, after which he is to serve four years on probation. Pete has three prior arrests related to felony drug offenses: one for possession of marijuana, one for possession of cocaine, and one for possession of marijuana with intent to distribute. He successfully completed a drug court program for the first possession of marijuana arrest, he successfully completed a three-year probationary term for the possession of cocaine conviction, and he was sentenced to six months in jail, followed by two years on probation, which he successfully completed for conviction for possession of marijuana with intent to distribute. All of these sentences resulted from plea agreements as did the current conviction which placed him in the halfway house. The program he is currently in is considered a "halfway in" program because it precedes any prison sentence, as opposed to "halfway out" which is a post-prison term.

Pete is a high school graduate with 16 hours completed of general education college-level course work for which he received an overall 3.2 GPA. He served a brief stint in the army (9 months) immediately after high school. He was medically discharged for asthma-related complications. Pete is currently single, having previously been married for two years and divorced five years ago. He has no children. Pete was living by himself prior to the recent sentence. He has been sporadically employed in construction throughout his adult life. He has never been on government assistance. Pete has lived in the same community where he was born except for the brief time he was in the army. He is a single child of parents who are still married and both working at a local automotive factory.

Hank is assigned to be Pete's halfway house case manager. In his initial meeting with Pete he was pleased to learn that Pete is personable, with excellent communication. Pete also expressed willingness to abide by the house rules, including gaining and maintaining employment within 30 days of placement and continuing employment throughout his stay. Although offenders are required to pay the halfway house the majority of their earnings, a portion is deposited in a savings account to establish independent living after release from the halfway house. The house provides Pete's transportation for employment.

If a resident is unable to comply with this rule, the case manager is required to submit a notice to the sentencing court. The judge then requires that the offender return to court for a decision on an appropriate course of action. Through previous experience, Hank knows the judge has lifted suspended sentences and imposed prison time, given the offender an additional 30 days to comply, sentenced the offender to jail time, imposed a short period of prison time followed by reinstatement in the halfway house, or ordered a combination of any one or more of these alternatives. The judge usually asks the halfway house case managers for a recommendation that, in most cases, he follows.

Unfortunately, Pete has been unable to find employment and the 30-day allowable period has expired. Pete sought employment opportunities with local construction companies, but with the downturn in the economy, few positions are available and he was not hired. Pete followed all of Hank's requirements for verification of employment applications and also applied to various fast food eateries and restaurants, but he has not secured a job offer. Because one requirement of the house is that residents inform prospective employers that they are sentenced offenders serving time in the area's halfway house, Hank is concerned that this requirement may be the reason for Pete's inability to find employment.

Pete gets along well with all other residents. He attends substance abuse sessions that are held at the house, he fulfills all work assignments at the house (such as janitorial services, food preparation and clean-up, and maintenance). In addition, all urine screens have indicated no alcohol or drug use.

Assignment 2.3

1. Based on the type of crime he was convicted of and his prior record, do you think that the sentence given Pete was appropriate? If you say "yes," what is your justification? If you say "no," what is the justification and what should Pete's sentence be? Provide a rationale.

2. Considering Pete's noncompliance with the employment regulation, what do you think Hank should recommend to the judge in the report he is required to file? How should he justify the recommendation?

3. Do you think there is any situation that a case manager could justify asking for a waiver of the employment requirement that would allow a resident to remain in the halfway house? What would that situation be? Be detailed in your explanation.

4. If you think that a waiver of the employment requirement is justifiable in some situations, what could be a negative consequence for the day-to-day operations of the halfway house? Explain.

5. Do you think that requiring residents to advise possible employers of their current offense status and sentence is a sound policy based on reasonable grounds? Explain your answer.

6. Do you think that Hank should confidentially advise Pete not to inform possible employers of his offense status and current sentence to the halfway house? Why or why not? What should be a consequence to Hank if he were to do this? Explain.

7. What should be included in Hank's case management plan for Pete? Include detailed goals with expected outcomes.

Work Release — Ralph

Ralph is a 52-year-old male recently transitioned to the state's work release center after having served 12 years for forcible rape, aggravated assault, and attempted murder of a 19-year-old convenience store clerk. The crime occurred at the store at approximately 2:00 a.m. when no customers were in the store. Although one other employee was to be on the premises at all times after midnight, the other scheduled worker went home sick that evening without a replacement being called. No robbery took place. Ralph was sentenced to 20 years for this offense but with good time was released from prison on condition that he spend one year in work release, followed by seven years on parole. Ralph has two prior felony convictions for aggravated assault, the first at age 26 for which he served nine months in the county jail and five years on probation (receiving a successful discharge) and the second at the age of 33 for which he was sentenced to four years of prison, serving two followed by two years on parole, which he successfully completed. These two prior aggravated assault convictions involved young adult females. Although no sexual assault charges were brought in these cases, there was some evidence that this was the intent. The prosecutor decided that the evidence gathered was not sufficient to press for attempted rape charges. Ralph had no arrests prior to age 26.

Ralph completed the ninth grade of high school and then dropped out, ran away from home, relocated to a larger neighboring city, and picked up odd jobs, living mainly on the streets and occasionally in homes of employers. He never returned to his family's home after leaving at the age of 14. He has one brother, age 46, who is currently serving a twenty-year sentence on a second degree murder conviction. Raised by his mother, who was never married to his father, Ralph stated in a previous evaluation that he does not know who his father is. During the prison evaluation at the Receiving and Diagnostic Center, Ralph stated that he was frequently physically and sexually abused by many of his mother's male visitors, the first occurrence when he was six. He stated that his brother was also abused. Ralph added that his mother "is a drunk" and that he and his brother often went hungry because she spent the government financial support she received "on herself, her booze, and her male companions." Ralph's psychological evaluation indicates no personality disorder and average intelligence. The report summarizes Ralph's outlook on life as "angry, filled with resentment, suspicious of every person he encounters, and filled with an intense dislike and distrust of females." The evaluator indicates that "it appears that Ralph goes out of his way to make people dislike him … this is likely due to his purposeful intent of creating situations where people will avoid him … he repeatedly stated that he doesn't like anyone."

Ralph has never been married and has made statements in various evaluations that he does not like women, he has no intent to change that position, and he is perfectly content being "a loner." Prison records indicate that he has no disciplinary actions for fighting with other inmates while incarcerated. He appears to have found a way to serve his sentence by completing work assignments, drawing, and using recreation time for weight lifting activities. He has not participated in any self-improvement programs such as education, vocational training, or counseling. Although his work details during the first three years of his incarceration involved cafeteria clean-up, he spent the last nine years working in the prison library, repairing books and checking material in and out to other inmates. For a person who attended the public school system only until the 9th grade, Ralph appears to have picked up advanced reading skills during his adult years. The corrections department's rationale for placing Ralph in work release is to provide him with close supervision in a residential setting and, at the same time, help him gain stable employment, thus leading to a positive transition to independent living while on parole.

Don is a case manager with five years of experience at the work release center where Ralph will reside during the coming year. In preparation for Ralph's transition from prison to the center, Don has spoken to numerous possible suitable employers for Ralph, considering the risk he could pose to the public. Don has sought inventory and stocking employment with bookstores. He thinks that a job that limits Ralph's contact with customers, allows him to stay in a familiar work duty, and uses his physical abilities for unloading shipments from trucks and moving merchandise where needed is advisable. Through his contacts, Don has determined that a large book retailer is willing to employ Ralph 30 hours a week, working from 6:00 p.m. to midnight, five days a week in inventory and stocking. He will have one supervisor during his work shift. The supervisor has worked with other convicted felons over the past seven years, has a reputation for exerting a good influence on the people he supervises, and makes reliable reports to the corrections department. Don has used the same employer with different positions a few other times. Furthermore, this bookstore is registered with the state as a stable employer of convicted felons, but this is the first time it will employ a person transitioning from prison. The bookstore has shown an interest in providing employment for convicted felons for two reasons: (1) one third of an employee's salary is paid for by the state, and (2) it has had positive experiences in hiring convicted felons in the past finding them to be highly dedicated, motivated and reliable employees. Even though Don has advised the supervisor of Ralph's criminal background, Ralph must complete an interview for the job and explain to the supervisor his criminal background and correctional involvement. Ralph knows of this condition and agreed to comply prior to being accepted into the work release program.

Six weeks after beginning his employment with the bookstore, Ralph tells Don that he needs to find another placement because he does not like his work supervisor because he constantly gives him pointers on how to turn his life around and "preaches religion to him." Don has received positive reports from Ralph's supervisor that Ralph is hard-working, methodical in fulfilling his job duties, and willing to accept direction. Nothing in the employment progress reports indicates that Ralph has presented any difficulties in his work performance, attitude toward his work, or following direction.

Assignment 2.4

1. What suggestions do you have for Don to address Ralph's discontent with his current employment placement? In your explanation describe potential consequences of the course you suggest Don should take, both positive and negative.

2. Do you think that states should offer employment incentives for employers to hire convicted felons? Why or why not?

3. Do you think that Don should discuss with Ralph's supervisor the advice he is giving Ralph specific to his religious beliefs? Provide a rationale for your position.

4. Do you think that the corrections department's decision to transition Ralph to work release was appropriate, based on his criminal background? Using examples from the case to provide the rationale for your position, explain your answer.

5. On a scale of 1 to 10, with 10 being the highest probability for successful completion of the work release program and 1 being the least likelihood for success, how do you rate the likelihood that Ralph will complete the one-year work release program? Explain your answer, using examples given in the case information to support your rating.

6. What other employment options fit Ralph's particular situation? Explain your answer.

7. Why do you think that Ralph is reacting as he is to his supervisor's comments? What suggestions should Don make to Ralph for

appropriately addressing Ralph's discontent with his supervisor's comments? Be detailed in your answer.

Residential Mental Health Placement — Linda

Linda is a 27-year-old female currently residing in a county-operated residential mental health facility. She was placed in the facility by order of a district court judge after review of police reports and reports from child protective services related to an arrest for child abuse and neglect. She has been in the facility for 12 days but has not been sentenced. The judge had ordered placement in the facility on the grounds that Linda is a danger to herself and others, in this case her two children ages 2 months and 18 months. A summary to the judge of the incident that led to Linda's arrest indicates that the police responded to a report from a neighbor concerned that Linda might hurt her children. The neighbor stated that Linda was acting in a bizarre manner, screaming obscenities, running in and out of the house clothed only in her undergarments, and pulling the 18-month-old child by the wrist, dragging him as she ran around the yard yelling incomprehensible words. Reports of the two officers who responded to the call verified the neighbor's account. The officers contacted child protective services, who sent an investigator to the scene. Linda was physically subdued and taken to the mental health ward of the local hospital for observation. Child protective services took immediate temporary custody of the two children, who were placed in a foster home where they have remained since Linda was removed from the home. Child abuse charges were filed by the prosecutor. After an initial evaluation conducted at the hospital, additional detailed psychological testing was ordered and Linda was transported to the mental health facility through the court order. On the night of the incident Linda's 18-month-old son was transported to the local hospital for evaluation and was diagnosed with a dislocated left arm at the elbow and at the shoulder joint. The infant was also evaluated and found to have severe diaper "burn" (an advanced form of diaper rash) with open sores in the genital area. Both children were malnourished.

Authorities later learned that Linda has been a patient of a local mental health outpatient provider on and off for the preceding eight years. Her records indicate a diagnosis of paranoid schizophrenia and an IQ of 54, indicating an intellectual disability. The mental health provider had had no contact with Linda for the previous eight months and was unaware that she had given birth to a second child. Linda originally came to the outpatient program by way of a referral by a case manager employed with the mental health court of the county after she was arrested for disturbing the peace and assaulting a police officer. Both charges were dropped after the prosecutor's office determined that Linda should be "diverted" from the criminal justice system to appropriate mental health services. This first encounter with the criminal justice system occurred eight years earlier when Linda was 19 years old. Since that time Linda was referred on three separate occasions to the mental health court as a result of encounters with the police after complaints called in to 911 that Linda was behaving bizarrely in public locations, twice at the mall and once at the post office. When Linda was evaluated by the psychiatrist after the initial referral through the mental health court, she was diagnosed as paranoid schizophrenic and prescribed psychotropic medications. The records from the mental health agency indicate that Linda had stopped taking the medications prior to each incident when she came to the attention of the criminal justice system and was processed through the mental health court. When Linda takes her medication, she functions well, attending counseling sessions, participating in group activities organized by the mental health agency, and working part-time for a second-hand clothing shop operated by a nonprofit organization. She lives with her two children in government-subsidized housing and covers independent living expenses by her employment earnings and Social Security payments she receives because of her mental illness. While she works she takes her son with her and has him cared for onsite at the daycare.

Before the most recent incident, Linda had not worked for several months. Because she told her employer she needed some time off due to her pregnancy, the employer had no reason to report her absence to anyone. When she ceased working, Linda was functional and her son was healthy and showed no signs of neglect or abuse. When Linda gave birth, she appeared able to care for the newborn. In the brief time that Linda was at the hospital, her son was cared for by a friend who lives in the same apartment complex as Linda and who is also a client of the mental health agency. Soon after she was discharged from the hospital, Linda's mental state became unstable.

Linda came to the community when she was 19 years old. She apparently has no family or support system in the area and no record of her past, including why she has located to the community, who to contact for assistance, what her level of education is, and whether she had prior employment. The only form of documentation Linda has is a Social Security card.

Because Linda has had previous encounters with the criminal justice system and the mental health court and because she physically injured her 18-month-old son and her baby had physical consequences of neglect, and she allowed both children to be malnourished, the judge has directed the prosecutor to pursue criminal charges for child abuse. As a result of this directive, the case will not be handled through the county mental health court but through the county district court.

Sue, a case manager who works in the prosecutor's office, is responsible for reviewing all reports on the client and the case and interviewing representatives of all the agencies involved in the current case, as well as those that have worked with Linda in the past or are currently providing a service to her. After gathering information from all sources, Sue is to write a summary report and submit a recommendation to the court. Because Sue has been in her current position for 11 years, she understands well the issue of confidentiality in reference to past and present mental health records. Although counselors', psychologists', and psychiatrists' notes cannot be reviewed, she can gather enough background information to make an informed recommendation to the court.

Assignment 2.5

1. Research information about mental health courts and write a 1- to-2 page paper on how these courts operate.

2. What agencies should Sue contact to gather background information? Be sure to cite information from Linda's case to provide reasons for any agency you note. What type of information should be gathered from these agencies?

3. Do you think that the judge should have directed the prosecutor to file charges in the district court, thus removing the case from the jurisdiction of the mental health court? Why or why not? Be sure to provide a detailed response and a rationale for your position.

4. Do you think the children should remain in foster care, or should they be returned to Linda's care? Explain your answer. If you say they should remain in foster care, how long should this go on? Should child protective services seek termination of parental rights so that the children can be eligible for adoption? Why or why not? If you say that they should be returned to Linda, what suggestions do you have for preventing continued abuse and/or neglect?

5. What type of intervention services do you think the judge should order in this case? Be detailed in your response.

6. If Linda is found guilty on the child abuse charges, what do you think is an appropriate sentence?

7. In what way could the child abuse and neglect have been prevented?

8. Do you think that anyone "dropped the ball" in this case, thus enabling the abuse? Explain your position.

Residential Substance Abuse Program — Jacob

Jacob is a 27-year-old male currently residing in a residential substance abuse program as the result of a plea agreement. He pled guilty to one count of possession of cocaine after his attorney informed him that if he did not plead guilty and agree to completing the six-month residential substance abuse program, the prosecutor would push for three years in prison. Jacob has six prior felony arrests for drug-related offenses: four arrests for possession of marijuana, one arrest for possession of drug paraphernalia, and one arrest for possession of illegally obtained prescription medications. In the prior arrests for possession of marijuana Jacob paid a fine to the court and completed community service. The arrest for possession of drug paraphernalia resulted in a sentence of 18 months of probation, which Jacob successfully completed. The possession of illegally obtained prescription medications resulted in a fine of $1,000 and 200 hours of community service, which Jacob successfully completed.

Jacob is a high school graduate with 75 hours of college credit completed toward a degree in computer science. He has sporadically been employed during his adulthood as a consultant with a locally owned computer programming business where he writes specialized software programs for a variety of local businesses. Jacob has resided with his parents throughout his adult life and has never lived independently. Both high school and college GPA's are 4.0. His parents are wealthy members of the local community.

Tim, who has seven years of experience, has been assigned to be Jacob's case manager at the residential treatment facility. After meeting individually with Jacob several times over the previous three weeks, Tim decides to bring some concerns about Jacob's demeanor to his supervisor, Ruth. Tim tells Ruth that Jacob's attitude toward treatment does not bode well for making positive decisions in the future about drug use. Jacob believes that his use of drugs is a personal choice that should not be illegal because he harms no one, he commits no illegal acts to obtain money to purchase the drugs, and he has always controlled what he uses and how it affects him. Tim explains that other residents thoroughly dislike Jacob because they perceive him as having an arrogant "rich boy" attitude. He is rude to others in group counseling, complains about their "whining," and uses derogatory nicknames when addressing others. Tim tells Ruth that he has addressed these issues several times with Jacob, but Jacob jokes about the situation and tells Tim he takes things "way too seriously," and furthermore he is not concerned with serving time in prison because his father has "influence." Jacob has admitted to using a variety of illegal drugs for which he was never caught and to starting marijuana use when he was twelve. He has also stated that police picked him up several times as a juvenile for being at parties with older friends where arrests were made for illegal drug possession and underage drinking. Rather than being referred to juvenile services, he was taken home.

Tim tells Ruth that he strongly believes that Jacob's drug use is much more serious, ingrained, and frequent than court documents reflect. He also explains to Ruth that he feels frustrated because he cannot get Jacob to recognize that he has an addiction to drugs that can result in negative consequences.

Assignment 2.6

1. Jacob has been in the residential treatment program for only three weeks. Did Tim take the correct action in bringing his concerns to his supervisor, or should he have waited a few more weeks to see if Jacob's attitude toward the program became more positive? Explain your rationale for your response.

2. If you were Tim's supervisor, what advice would you give him regarding how best to address Jacob's apparent lack of interest in taking the treatment seriously?

3. The court ordered Jacob to complete the drug treatment program successfully. Do you think that the sentencing judge should be advised of Jacob's poor adjustment to treatment? Explain your rationale for your response.

4. Part of the treatment program is involvement of family members. What approach should Tim use with Jacob's parents? What could be possible consequences for Jacob for the approach that you suggest?

5. What could be a turning point (a catalyst) in Jacob's treatment that would motivate him to become more positively involved in the treatment process?

6. What message do you think Jacob received through his previous involvements with the criminal justice system? What do you think

should have been done in these previous incidents that could have reduced the chance that Jacob would be where he is at today?

7. The information contained in this case study indicates that some offenders receive preferential treatment. Do you think this occurs frequently? What is the basis for your answer? How would you ensure that all offenders are treated equally by decision makers of the criminal justice system (police, courts, and corrections)?

Chapter Three

Community Corrections

Introduction

The focus of this chapter is on various adult community corrections options that can be part of an offender's sentence. After each case study questions are provided to serve as discussion points, homework assignments, topics for individual or group in-or out-of-class activities, and quiz and/or test subject matter. The questions encourage the reader to reflect on a variety of issues as presented in the facts of each case. The reader should thoroughly consider the issues presented and apply information learned in previous courses, knowledge of the criminal justice system (such as through employment and awareness of current events), review of research, and personal awareness, where appropriate. There are many community corrections intervention options available. The chapter focuses on six cases: (1) an offender sentenced to *probation* for property and drug offenses, (2) an offender returning to the community on *parole* after serving prison time for a violent offense, (3) an offender returning to the community on *electronic monitoring* after having served prison time for a sex offense, (4) a young man with mental health challenges attending a *day treatment program* who had been convicted of property offenses, (5) a young female offender serving probation time under *house arrest* after being convicted of drug crimes, and (6) a young male offender sentenced to a *drug court program*.

Case Studies

Probation — Bill

Jane, a county adult probation officer, receives a notice from her supervisor that she will be assigned a new client, Bill, who has been sentenced to time already served in jail, followed by three years supervised probation, for residential burglary and possession of marijuana convictions. Because Bill was not bailed out after his arrest, he has spent 67 days in the county jail. The sentence results from a plea agreement. His probation begins on January 18.

Bill's file shows that he has one prior arrest for marijuana possession three years earlier. He was given a deferred sentence and ordered to complete the county drug court program after which, if successfully discharged, the charges for marijuana possession would be dismissed. Records indicate that Bill was successfully discharged after having completed all three levels of the program over a seventeen-month period. During the first four months, however, three urine screens tested positive for cannabis. All subsequent urine screens (a total of 27) indicated no use of alcohol or other illegal drugs.

Information about the current charge (residential burglary) indicates that Bill, along with two other adult males who are co-defendants in this case, was charged with burglarizing a residence at 2:38 a.m. on November 12. A home security silent alarm notified the local police department of a break-in at the residence at which point police were dispatched to the location. Upon arrival at the residence Bill, along with the two others, were seen exiting the rear door of the residence with electronic equipment in hand, including a laptop computer, a game system, and a portable stereo system. All three men stopped at police command, set the items on the ground, and followed police orders. At this point they were arrested and taken to the county jail. All three were also found to be in possession of marijuana, Bill having a baggie filled with four ounces in his front pants pocket.

Bill is a 24-year-old white male with a tenth grade education (no GED). At the time of arrest he was residing with a maternal aunt and uncle with whom he has lived sporadically over the past four years. During the times he did not live with them, he had many address changes, moving on average every six weeks, living with a variety of acquaintances both male and female. He has been employed in temporary hourly positions in construction and roofing without benefits. Tax records show that Bill earned an average of $11,000 annually over the past three years.

After completing a risk and needs assessment, Jane determines that Bill should be placed on maximum probation supervision for a minimum of six months after which time a reassessment will be conducted to determine if his supervision level should remain maximum or be reduced. The determination for maximum supervision is based on the following risk factors:

Unstable employment
Undereducated
Unstable housing arrangements
Prior felony record
Increased level of seriousness in crime involvement
Second felony drug offense
Prior felony court jurisdiction

Assignment 3.1

Develop a case management plan based on the risk factors noted above. Include specific information regarding goals to be accomplished and time for achieving the goals. To develop a case management plan, you need to start by identifying the main goal(s) that Bill must strive to achieve while on probation. For each goal, at least one objective must be identified. For example, if a main goal is to obtain gainful employment within 30 days of the start of probation, one objective can be to complete a minimum of five applications a week. Another objective can be enrollment in a free government operated employment service (usually offered through or in collaboration with the state employment commission) within five days of the start of probation. A subset of objectives related to participation in this service may include the following: (1) provide the probation officer with documentation of type of service participation, along with date and activity of service, and (2) keep a log of all activities related to participation in service activities, including a description of what was gained through involvement. Include detailed instructions in the plan so that Bill can clearly understand what is expected of him. For each objective, include the date for expected completion. Allow space after this date for Jane, the probation officer, to indicate whether and when the objective was completed or why the objective was not completed.

Parole — Brian

Jim, a state adult parole officer with twelve years of experience, receives information from his supervisor that he is assigned supervision of Brian on parole after his release from prison which will occur any time in the next six weeks. Jim is familiar with the file information because Jim was the officer who completed the parole plan check out on Brian's case.

Brian, a 34-year-old male, has served seven years of a sixteen-year sentence for aggravated robbery. He was found guilty through a jury trial that lasted three weeks and took the jury over seven hours to reach a decision. A summary of the court documents indicates that Brian robbed a convenience store clerk at knife point, leaving the scene with $142 in cash and a case of beer. A description of Brian and his vehicle was called in by the store clerk and confirmed by three separate witnesses who were also in the store when it was robbed. A public service announcement resulted in an anonymous tip called in to the police emergency line that Brian, who appeared to be intoxicated, could be located at a city park. At the park the police encountered a subject fitting the description put out on the police All Points Bulletin and the vehicle Brian allegedly used. Witnesses at the park stated that they saw a male, later identified as Brian, jump off the side of a bridge over a deep, fast-running river that ran through the park. A boater, seeing Brian struggling in the water, jumped in and pulled him to shore. Brian later stated to the police that he jumped in an attempt to drown himself. His blood alcohol content was .28. A blood test confirmed no illegal drug use.

The records indicate that Brian has four prior DUI arrests, for which he successfully completed six months of supervised probation, a 30 day inpatient treatment program, and six months in the county jail. No other arrests are indicated.

Brian's wife filed for divorce three months after he entered prison. Brian has two minor children from this marriage, currently ages nine and eleven, both males. His ex-wife has since remarried and moved to a state 1,500 miles away from where Brian will be paroled. Statements made by Brian's ex-wife at the time of sentencing indicate a pattern of domestic violence linked to his drinking, but since no police reports were made, that information is unconfirmed.

Brian had been employed for approximately two years in a plumbing apprenticeship program as part of the vocational school program he attended prior to the arrest that resulted in his prison sentence. He was more than half way through the program. The supervisor of the program attended his sentencing hearing and testified to Brian's strong work ethic and good school performance. When the judge asked what he thought the sentence should be, the supervisor indicated a period of probation.

Prison records show that Brian has had two prior psychological evaluations, one during the first six months of his prison sentence and one after an attempted suicide six years later when Brian attempted to hang himself in his cell. The first evaluation resulted in a diagnosis of alcohol dependence, but no personality disorders, and an average intelligence. The second evaluation resulted in a diagnosis of major depression. Brian completed a vocational program in heating, venting, and air conditioning while incarcerated and has been certified in HVAC. Brian has a high school diploma.

As a veteran state parole officer, Jim knows the regulations for clearing a prisoner for parole release when he/she is within six months of a scheduled release date. After getting information on Brian's plans for residence and employment during his parole, Jim went to the home address listed on the parole plan to talk with Brian's maternal grandmother, Mrs. Carter, age 86. Jim discovered that both of Brian's parents died in an automobile accident when Brian was 26 years old. Brian's grandmother explained that the car accident resulted from her son-in-law's drinking and driving. She confirmed that Brian can live with her until "he gets his feet on the ground," but then she expects him to find his own place to live. Although she agrees to let Brian live with her for a limited period, she is concerned that Brian has the "same drinking problem his father had" and she "wants no part of it." Jim verified with the employer listed on the parole plan, a local construction company, that Brian has secured temporary employment upon release from prison and that his continued employment with the company will depend on his work performance.

Assignment 3.2

1. Create a list of what you view as the risks of Brian's successfully completing his parole, listing risk factors by significance, starting with the factor you think presents the greatest risk to Brian's successful completion of parole.

2. Create a list of needs that should be included in a case management plan for Brian. Prioritize what you think is the most significant need by listing that need first on the list.

3. On a scale of 1 to 10, with 1 being most likely to complete parole successfully and 10 being very unlikely to successfully complete parole, how do you rate Brian's chances of successfully completing parole? Explain your answer by stating the basis for your rating.

4. What community resources do you think are crucial to assist Brian throughout his parole? Explain your answer by identifying specific case history details that each resource can address.

Electronic Monitoring — Doug

Mary, an adult probation and parole officer with two years experience, has recently been assigned what she is quickly discovering is a very difficult case. Doug has already served 18 months of a five-year parole term and has recently been transferred to Mary's caseload after his parole officer resigned. The officer that resigned, a female in her early thirties, had been on the job for approximately four years.

Doug served 10 years in prison on a 5-to-20 year sentence for forcible rape. Doug has four prior arrests for assault and battery, one prior arrest for simple battery, and one prior arrest for intimidation. After reviewing the case files on these prior arrests, Mary discovers that none resulted in prosecution because the victims withdrew their complaints. Police records indicate that each incident involved a different female victim, each one a previous college classmate or co-worker of the offender. In reading the police reports, Mary recognized a pattern. A common denominator in all complaints was that Doug "does not take no for an answer." All complainants indicated that Doug at first was very charming, and all felt he was a good "friend," but the longer they knew him, the more controlling he became and the more aggressively he sought their attention. When they tried to disengage from any relationship with him, he became more insistent that they pay attention only to him. The assault and battery complaints resulted from Doug's grabbing an arm, a wrist, or a shoulder and not letting go when the complainants told him the physical contact was unwelcome. In all of the cases an outside party intervened to help the women escape from Doug's grasp when the women vocalized their discomfort/fear with the contact. All of these encounters occurred in highly public areas.

In reviewing the prison records, Mary discovers that Doug lost good time credits (a total of three years) due to physical encounters he had with male and female staff. None of the disciplinary reports stemmed from encounters between Doug and other inmates, and none of the reports resulted from physical encounters between Doug and correctional officers; the staff filing complaints was counselors and educators. Although no incidents involved physical contact, they stemmed from Doug being "verbally assaultive." In three of the reports the word "intimidation" was used. Because of his prior arrests and complainant interactions, the violent nature of his current offense, and his disciplinary reports while incarcerated, a condition of his release is that he will be monitored electronically during the first two years of his parole.

Having read all of this information in Doug's file prior to her initial meeting with him, Mary is surprised to encounter a soft-spoken, polite, and well-groomed man with above-average communication skills and a good sense of humor. Reports from the agency contracted to oversee compliance with the electronic monitoring requirements indicate that he has not been in violation. Doug is required to be at his residence, where he lives with his mother, or at his place of employment, where he works at a fast food restaurant as a cook. He is not permitted to frequent known liquor establishments or be in any public location other than his place of employment. He walks from home to work, as neither he nor his mother has access to a vehicle. His residence and place of employment are only a half mile apart. Doug does not have a current driver's license.

Doug is required to report weekly to his parole officer, to complete a reporting form, and have contact with his parole officer. The parole office operates on a first-come-first-serve basis since it does not schedule appointments with clients. Seldom is a client required to wait longer than an hour to see his/her parole officer.

After meeting with Doug weekly for two months, Mary begins to sense a change in Doug's conversations with her. Although she persists in her attempts to keep the communications with Doug focused on his parole compliance, he frequently interrupts her to ask questions about her educational background, her interest in pursuing higher education, and her reasons for going into parole work. Several times she has told him to leave her office because she had work to do and clients to visit. She has recently worked out a system with the receptionist to buzz her office after five minutes to tell her she has a client waiting, whether she does or not. Two days earlier, she thought she saw Doug lingering outside the parole office when she was ready to leave for the day. She was concerned enough to go back into the office to get another officer to walk her to her car. When she returned to the parking lot, she did not see Doug.

Because she knows his background, Mary thinks that she may be making too much of Doug's actions and reading too much into her conversations with him. Part of her wants to talk with her supervisor, but another part does not want anyone to think she cannot handle the job. Although she has recently completed her probationary employment period, she believes that if she indicates in any way that she has concerns about being Doug's parole officer, she will be evaluated poorly on her next review. The parole office where Mary works has a policy of not transferring clients from one officer to another except for the resignation or relocation of an officer.

Assignment 3.3

1. What is the name of the type of sentencing used in Doug's case?

2. Does Mary have legitimate concerns for personal safety as a result of her interactions thus far with Doug? Name at least two indicators that are "red flags" for Mary's safety.

3. Do you think Mary should talk with her supervisor about her concerns in working with Doug? Explain your answer.

4. If Mary were to talk about her concerns with her supervisor what advice and/or action do you think the supervisor should give/take about Mary's concerns in working with Doug?

5. Do you agree or disagree with the office policy that clients cannot be transferred to another officer unless the officer resigns or relocates? Explain your answer. If you think the policy is warranted, what suggestions do you have for dealing with the challenges Mary is facing? If you think the policy should be changed, what suggestions do you have for changes?

6. If you were the parole officer assigned to take over Doug's case, what would be your case management plan? The plan must include a description of frequency of contact, time length for each "stage" of parole supervision, a minimum of three goals that you encourage Doug to complete within three years of his parole, and a list of "rewards" for goal achievement, as well as consequences for failure to achieve each goal.

Day Treatment Program — Frank

Frank is a 26-year-old male who was court ordered to serve three years on probation for five counts of felony larceny over $500. The summary of the offenses, as stated in the presentencing report, indicates that Frank stole game systems and video games from five separate stores over an eight-month period. After the police department raided a storage unit based on a tip from an informant that the unit was used as a distribution center for stolen goods, mainly electronics, the police arrested seven adult males and charged them with receiving and distribution of stolen merchandise. Information from one of these individuals led to the arrest of 22 additional adult males, separately charged with larceny and/or distribution. Serial numbers on the game systems were traced to stores from which they were stolen and dates of theft. Information subsequently led to the questioning of Frank who, after waiving Miranda, confessed to stealing the game systems as well as numerous video games and selling the items to others at the storage unit.

Frank dropped out of school during the eighth grade. Along with numerous extended family members, he worked in the fields during harvesting. Although he has citizenship in the US, many of his family members do not. His family usually relocates to Mexico during the winter months, returning for spring, summer, and the first part of fall for field work. They travel between several counties for available work. Frank has never lived away from his parents and siblings.

Information in the presentencing report indicates that Frank's public defender had asked for a psychological evaluation prior to sentencing because he suspected that Frank was developmentally disabled. Test results indicated that Frank has an IQ of 64. Thus, it is likely that he would encounter difficulties assuming the responsibilities of independent living. Frank's mother indicated that Frank suffered an illness with a "high fever" over several days when he was four years old. Medical care was not sought. Frank's mother states that the family looks out for him because he "can't look out for himself." She expressed a concern that other boys have always taken advantage of him, getting him into trouble by telling him to steal things they wanted.

The plea agreement that led to the sentence of probation included a condition that Frank attend a day treatment program for individuals with developmental delays. Other special conditions for probation include prohibiting Frank from associating with other known felons and frequenting liquor establishments.

Jerry has been assigned to be Frank's probation officer. Although Jerry agrees with the basic premise of the probation conditions, he is concerned that having Frank attend the day reporting program will be difficult when the family depends on the work of all family members to earn a living. In addition, the family's lack of permanent residence is likely to present difficulties in complying with this condition. However, Jerry explains the requirement to Frank and his mother and father and emphasizes the seriousness of the situation. He also arranges for Frank to start a day treatment program that will transport him to and from his home to the program location every day.

One or both of Frank's parents bring him to the probation office for reporting as required. Urine screens indicate no alcohol or illegal drug use. After supervising Frank's probation for two months and checking with the case manager at the day treatment program, Jerry determines that Frank is doing well in the program, complying with all rules, and participating in the small appliance repair training program. Jerry feels more positive about Frank's chances to be able to fulfill the probation conditions successfully.

Four months into Frank's probation, Jerry gets a call from the case manager at the day treatment program, informing him that Frank has not attended the program for the past three days because he is reportedly ill. When Jerry goes to the family's residence to inquire about Frank's illness, he discovers that the parents have not seen Frank for five days (since the previous Friday). They allegedly have no idea where he has gone. After questioning the mother for more information, Jerry discovers that Frank told his mother that people were making fun of him on the transport bus and at the program and that he didn't want to go to the program anymore. The parents tell Jerry that they did not call him to report Frank's disappearance because they did not want him to get into trouble with the court. They further report that they are concerned that Frank may be hanging out with people who will get him into trouble. However, they claim not to know who that might be or where to find Frank. They go on to say that they plan to leave the area soon, and will leave without Frank if he does not return home by the following week.

Assignment 3.4

1. As Frank's probation officer, what is Jerry's obligation to the court?

2. Do you think that Jerry's responsibility extends to trying to locate Frank? Explain your answer.

3. If Frank returns home and reports in with his parents to Jerry's office within the next three days, how should Jerry deal with Frank's failure to attend the day reporting program? Should Jerry file a probation violation report because Frank has not been attending the program? If Jerry has already notified the court of Frank's failure to comply with probation conditions for attendance at the day reporting program, should Jerry recommend that Frank be continued on probation, or should Jerry recommend that Frank's probation be revoked? Explain the reasoning for your answer.

4. Do you think that Jerry should discuss what Frank's mother has told him about Frank's reason for not attending the program with the case manager who has been working with Frank? Explain your answer.

5. What suggestions do you have for addressing the issue that the family is intending to relocate and Frank has no one else to live with other than his family?

6. Do you think that the special probation conditions required of Frank are appropriate, based on his family circumstances? Explain your answer.

7. Should barriers for successful completion of special probation conditions be taken into consideration by the probation officer when deciding whether or not to notify the court of noncompliance? Explain your answer.

8. Do you think that Jerry should ask the court for a modification of Frank's condition to attend the day reporting program based on his family's relocation? Explain your answer.

9. What do you think the reason is for the court's ordering attendance at a day reporting program as a special condition? Do you think it is a reasonable condition? Explain your answer.

House Arrest — Cindy

Cindy is a 24-year-old female who has been sentenced to five years of probation as a result of a felony conviction of seven counts of distribution of a controlled substance, cocaine. The summary of the offense, as stated in the presentencing report, indicates that Cindy was part of a drug sale operation. Police investigations, summarized in the presentencing report, indicate that Cindy collaborated with her brothers in distributing cocaine to buyers known to her brothers. A buyer was instructed to drop off customer's cash and pick up cocaine in the requested amount at a locker location in a community-run fitness club. One of Cindy's brothers made the drop in the locker and Cindy watched for pick up and notified her brother, who then followed the buyer to determine his/her place of residence or employment. After Cindy checked the locker for the money, if the buyer took the cocaine and did not leave cash, the buyer was later contacted and threatened with exposure to the police unless he or she deposited twice the previously agreed upon amount of cash. Cindy and the customers never had personal contact. Cindy and her brothers' involvement in the illegal operation was discovered when an informant tipped off the police. A staged undercover operation revealed Cindy's involvement in the drug distribution.

Cindy has no prior arrests as either a juvenile or adult, and there are no indications of current or past drug use. Her connection to the drug market comes through contacts made by her two older brothers, ages 27 and 29, who both have prior felony arrests for possession of marijuana and cocaine. Both have served jail time and have been on probation. The older brother is currently serving a five-year prison sentence for his involvement in the drug operation. The other brother is currently in jail with charges pending in connection with their drug operation. Cindy has no other siblings. Both of her parents are deceased, having died three years earlier in a traffic accident.

Cindy is divorced with custody of three children, ages 6, 4, and 2. Because she is unemployed and has no employment history, she has been supporting herself and her children through government assistance programs. She is a high school graduate with an Associate's degree in computer science from the local junior college. Her ex-husband, who has never paid court-ordered child support, has a warrant for his arrest. He has had no contact with Cindy or the children since the divorce and she states she does not know his current location.

Cindy stated in the presentencing report that she has sought employment at a variety of locations but the wages she could earn do not equal the amount of money she gets from government assistance. She stated that she became involved in drug sales for the money. She stated that she planned to save what money she made from drug sales until she had $100,000 and then relocate to another state, buy a house, continue her education in computer science, and go to work for a computer company after all of her children were in school full-time. She prefers to be a stay-at-home mom until the children are all in school. She believes that it is best for the children that she raise them, not some daycare facility.

The recommendation of the probation officer in the presentencing report is for Cindy to receive probation with a stipulation of six months' house arrest. The sentencing judge followed the recommendations in the report. Factors cited in the report to justify the recommendation are as follows:

- Custodial parent of three young children with no probable alternative placement other than foster care if Cindy were to be sentenced to prison or jail
- Lack of prior arrests
- Lack of evidence of current or prior drug usage

- Evaluation report by a counselor with Child Protective Services asserting no indications of past or present abuse or neglect; that the children are well cared for and well-adjusted

Assignment 3.5

1. Do you think that the probation sentence is appropriate in this case? Provide a rationale for your position. If you think that the sentence is not appropriate, what should the sentence have been? Explain your answer.

2. Do you think that house arrest is appropriate as a special condition of probation in this case? If you respond yes, what is the value of having this as a special condition? If you respond no, why is it not an appropriate special condition? What do you think was the goal of the court by ordering house arrest? What purpose could house arrest serve in this case?

3. Do you think an offender's family responsibilities should be taken into consideration in sentencing? Why or why not?

4. Do you think that a male offender who is convicted of seven counts of distribution of a controlled substance and is the sole financial support of three young children through legitimate employment would receive the same sentence? Why or why not?

5. As Cindy's probation officer, would you rate her as maximum, medium, or minimal risk for probation violation? What are your criteria for making this determination?

6. As Cindy's probation officer, how often would you require face-to-face contact during the first six months of her probation? Explain your reasoning.

7. What should be the case management plan for Cindy for the first six months of her probation? Be sure to identify clear, specific goals, set benchmark objectives, and include a time frame for expected objective achievement.

County Drug Court Program — Phil

Phil is a 27-year-old male who has been court ordered to complete the County Drug Court Program as a result of an arrest for possession of methamphetamine. His placement in the program was initiated by the public defender representing him and agreed to by the county prosecutor. Phil has been told that if he receives a successful discharge from the program, the charges against him will be dismissed. The average length of program participation is 18 months, consisting of three stages, intensive, intermediate, and transitional. The number of urine screens administered depends on the case. Participants pay a service fee of $100 per week to be in the program and pay $15 for each screen ordered. Failure to pay does not result in removal from the program but, instead, results in an unsuccessful discharge and initiation of collection proceedings. Participants can be removed from the program prior to completion due to (1) any new misdemeanor or felony arrest, (2) failure to comply with required attendance in counseling and education sessions, (3) failure to meet with the program staff, as directed, and/or (4) repeated indications of continued illegal drug or alcohol use.

Phil is currently employed as an assistant manager in the retail business at a men's clothing store where he has been employed for the past five years. He has earned a high school diploma and 92 credits toward his Bachelor's in Business Management degree. He is single and has never been married and is engaged to be married within the year to a woman he has been cohabitating with over the past four years. He does not have children.

Phil has two prior DUI arrests for which he paid his fines and had a suspended license for one year. He also has one prior arrest for possession of marijuana, but the charges were dropped. In reference to the current charge of possession of methamphetamine, police reports indicate that after Phil was stopped for suspected DUI and ordered out of the vehicle, a glassine baggie of methamphetamine dropped out of his coat pocket. Because the breathalyzer test registered .06, he was not charged with DUI. However, he was arrested for possession of methamphetamine.

Betty, a case manager of the Drug Court Program, has been supervising Phil's case for the past three months. Since he is in the intensive level of the program, he must report to her weekly, submit to random alcohol and drug screening, attend educational sessions weekly, and attend group counseling sessions every other week. The case file indicates that Phil has paid his service and urine screen fees on time, has missed one weekly reporting session due to illness, and has attended all educational sessions, but he has missed six of the group counseling sessions, half of the number he should have attended. Upon entry into the program, Phil's urine screen tested positive for marijuana. Of a total of 27 urine screens, 7 tested positive for alcohol during the first three weeks of Phil's participation in the program. Subsequent screens show him to be alcohol and drug free.

Betty must submit weekly reports to the Court about Phil's compliance with the program rules. In the latest report, Betty has recommended that Phil be ordered to reappear before the Drug Court judge because of his failure to comply with the requirement to attend group counseling sessions. In the report, Betty indicates the progress made in discontinuation of alcohol and drug use, as indicated by the 20 negative urine screens over the past 9 weeks and Phil's compliance with meeting with her as scheduled, attending the educational sessions, and meeting the financial requirements. Betty notes in the report that Phil told her his reasons for not attending the group counseling sessions: (1) he does not like the other participants, (2) he does not have anything to say at the sessions, (3) he feels uncomfortable being in the sessions, and (4) he is not getting anything out of the sessions.

As the program description states, the judge can choose any one or a combination of the following alternatives:

- Leave the program requirements the same and warn Phil that he must comply with the requirements or the judge will impose a consequence
- Adjust the requirements, such as lift the requirement for attendance in group counseling, change the requirement to individual counseling, increase the required number of sessions,

increase the number of meetings with the case manager, order attendance in court to observe various court sentencing, etc.
- Order Phil to complete a certain number of community service hours as a consequence for his noncompliance
- Order Phil to serve one or more days in jail
- Terminate Phil from the program and take the case through to adjudication

Assignment 3.6

1. What is the name of the type of sentence that Phil received that originally placed him in the Drug Court Program?

2. Research information about drug court programs. Using three citations, write a brief summary of the basic components of the programs and their operating procedures.

3. Based on what you have learned about drug court programs in general, is Phil a "typical" candidate for drug court? Explain your answer, citing specifics about Phil's background.

4. Do you think that Betty took the appropriate action in notifying the drug court judge of Phil's failure to comply with the requirement for the group counseling sessions? Explain your answer. Would you have taken the same action if you were Phil's case manager? Explain your answer.

5. What should the judge decide, based on the recent report Betty has filed? Explain your answer, providing a rationale for your position.

6. Do you think that Phil's reasons for noncompliance with the requirement to attend group counseling sessions are legitimate? Explain your answer.

7. What alternatives do you suggest to gain Phil's compliance? Be detailed in your suggestions, including why you think they could accomplish the goal of compliance.

Chapter Four

Juvenile Intervention Services

Introduction

The focus of this chapter is on the various dispositions a judge may use in juvenile cases including social service interventions that may be requirements under the disposition orders. After each case study a list of questions is provided as discussion points, homework assignments, topics for individual or group in- or out-of-class activities, and quiz and/or test subject matter. The objective of the questions is to encourage the reader to reflect on the issues presented in the facts of each case. The reader is encouraged to consider thoroughly the issues presented and apply information learned in courses, knowledge of the criminal justice system (such as through employment and awareness of current events), review of research, and personal awareness, where appropriate. Of the many intervention options available to juvenile social service and court personnel, this chapter focuses on six case studies that illustrate some: (1) First Offender Program, (2) Family Intervention Services, (3) Substance Abuse Program, (4) Detention Facility Placement, (5) Correctional Placement, and (6) Aftercare Services.

Case Studies

First Offender Program — Scott

Scott is a 14-year-old male who has been ordered by the juvenile court judge to successfully complete the county's First Offender Program (FOP). This order results from a petition filed with the county Juvenile Probation Department after a referral from the local high school guidance counselor, based on Scott's repeated truancy, and a referral from the local city police department as the result of possessing alcohol as a minor.

After only two months of his freshman year of high school, Scott has been truant for more than one third of the school days. When he has attended, he has been tardy over half the time. The first quarter grade report reflects failing grades in all six classes.

One month earlier police were dispatched to a local city park after receiving a complaint about loud music from a resident in the area. Upon arrival, the police found over 40 youths, ranging in age from 12 to 16, gathered in the park, many of them in possession of beer and other alcoholic beverages. After police reports from this incident were forwarded to the juvenile probation department, various actions were taken, based on individual circumstances. In Scott's case the juvenile probation department filed a petition with the court, based on the charge that he was a minor in possession of alcohol and the report of truancy and failing grades from the school.

Three weeks after the FOP weekly sessions begin, a facilitator of the group that Scott is assigned notifies the juvenile probation office that Scott has missed the previous two sessions. Records indicate that he attended the first session without a parent or custodial guardian present, in violation of the requirement that at least one parent or custodial guardian attend each session with him. Since a parent or custodial guardian signed an agreement to abide by this requirement at the time of disposition, Jill, the juvenile probation officer assigned to Scott's case, decides to conduct a home visit. Scott's file indicates that he resides with his biological mother and step-father, along with his younger biological sister, age 11, and step-brother, age 17. Scott's father died of a heart attack when Scott was 10. Scott's mother remarried six months ago.

When Jill makes contact with Scott's mother during the home visit, Scott's step-father is at work. Scott's mother explains that neither she nor her husband feels responsible for attending the first offender sessions. When Jill reminds her that they signed to this requirement at the time of Scott's court disposition, she explains that her husband and she agreed that Scott has to suffer the consequences for his decisions and that they should not have to make time to involve themselves in the FOP. Scott's mother expresses similar lack of interest in Scott's truancy and failing grades. She reaffirmations that "Scott is responsible for his own decisions in life." Scott's mother repeats that Scott needs to be held responsible for decisions that he makes, including possession of alcohol.

Jill leaves the family home, frustrated over the discussion with Scott's mother and unsure of what to do next.

Assignment 4.1

1. Based on the case information, do you think that Scott is an appropriate candidate for a First Offender Program? Explain your answer, providing specific information from the case that supports your position.

2. Based on information available in the case study, what do you think may have triggered Scott's delinquent behavior?

3. The information presented in the case indicates that referrals to the juvenile probation office came from two sources. What two agencies made the referrals? What is the basis for the referrals — delinquent acts, status offenses, or both?

4. Should Jill gather any additional information relevant to Scott's case prior to deciding about the most appropriate action to take to address Scott's failure to comply with the disposition requirement to attend the First Offender Program? If you think that more information is needed, what and from whom should she collect information?

5. If you were the supervising juvenile probation officer, would you notify the juvenile court of Scott's failure to comply with the requirement to attend the First Offender Program? Why or why not?

6. If notification of Scott's failure to comply with disposition requirements results in the juvenile court judge asking for a recom-

mendation of what should occur, what would you suggest? Explain your answer.

7. Do you think that Scott's mother and/or step-father should be ordered to answer to the juvenile court for their failure to attend the FOP sessions with Scott? Explain your answer.

8. What suggestions would you make to increase the probability that Scott can successfully complete juvenile probation requirements? Be sure to be detailed in your response, including what can encourage positive outcomes in all areas that appear to be problematic for Scott, such as school attendance and grades, alcohol involvement, and family relations.

Family Intervention Program — The Green Family

The Green family consists of a mother and father and four biological children, ages 10, 12, 14, and 16, all females. Both parents work outside the home from 8 to 5, Monday through Friday, the mother as a librarian in the county library and the father as a laboratory technician at the local hospital.

The Green family has been referred to a community counseling agency for family intervention services by the family court. The parents were charged with felony neglect as a result of investigations conducted by the police and later by Child Protective Services. The local school system reported to the police that two of the children, ages 14 and 16, told a school official that they had been living with a friend after their parents changed the locks on the family home and told them they were no longer welcome to live there.

Interviews with the parents determined that they are extremely frustrated with their two older daughters for frequent truancy from school, curfew violations, poor grades, promiscuous sexual behavior, and alcohol use. The parents stated that all four children steal from them, taking money from their wallets and purses without permission and taking alcohol from the home. Both parents expressed frustration and indignation that their own children behave so disrespectfully after they have "given them everything they ever wanted." When asked to explain this statement, the parents indicated that they buy the girls the latest in electronics and clothes, spending thousands of dollars on each child at the beginning of every school year for new wardrobes and purchasing each girl the latest in cell phone technology. When asked about forcing the children to leave the house and changing the locks, both parents said they wanted to teach the girls a lesson. When asked whether the girls would be welcome back into the home the parents both said that they are not welcome to return until they agree to live by the rules of the house: (1) no grade lower than a B and zero reports of truancy, (2) curfew of 9:00 p.m. on school nights and 10:00 p.m. on weekends and holidays, (3) no alcohol use, and (4) no stealing money or alcohol from the home. The parents added that if the girls do not agree to these rules, then they are not welcome to return home and they, the parents, would rather suffer the consequences of the court than "have the older two girls ruin the younger ones that are still living at home."

Interviews with the two younger children revealed little. Both appeared confused over the attention given to them by strangers and provided mainly monosyllable responses or no responses to questions posed. The older two children were very vocal in expressing their opinions and answering the questions of both the investigating police officer and the child protective service investigator. Both girls accused their parents of always being out to get them and not caring about their own children. They say their parents care only about themselves. The girls stated that their parents frequently leave them for two or three days at a time to take "mini vacations" and that they are expected to take care of their younger siblings. They also stated that their parents frequently entertain adult guests in the home and often "get drunk" on these occasions. The girls expressed a great deal of resentment toward their parents and stated that they never intend to live with them again, that they are happier living at their friends' homes.

Interviews with school personnel confirm that the two older daughters have frequently been truant and have failed the majority of their classes during the current school year but had marginally passing grades in the previous three years.

Beth, a social worker and licensed family therapist employed with the county family court, has been assigned the Green case. The family court judge has expressed a preference to divert this case out of the criminal justice system as long as the parents and the two older daughters agree to participate in individual and group counseling. The judge has met with Beth, Mr. and Mrs. Green, and the two older daughters and informed everyone that he will review a report from Beth after six months of intervention and decide at that time as to whether or not to dismiss the charges of neglect.

Assignment 4.2

1. Did the judge make the appropriate choice? If your response is affirmative, why do you think this is an appropriate decision? If you disagree with the judge's choice, explain what you think is a more appropriate decision. Be sure to use information from the case to provide a rationale for your response.

2. What actions should Beth incorporate into the intervention plan? Be sure to be detailed in the plan you suggest, including referrals for services you think are appropriate. Prioritize the actions you suggest and explain your reasoning.

3. Do you think that the Green family should meet for interventions as a group, individual sessions, or possibly some combination of both approaches? Explain the reasoning for your response.

4. Do you think that Beth should act as the sole provider of counseling sessions to all the Green family members, or should Beth be the primary counselor for either the parents or the children and another family therapist serve the other family members? In your response to this question take a position and present your response as a debate, presenting the pros and cons of both approaches.

5. Do you think the older daughters are justified in resenting their parents? Use information from the case to provide a rationale for your answer.

6. Do you think that the parents' approach to "teach the girls a lesson" is appropriate? Why or why not? What would you do if confronted with a similar situation?

7. Do you think there is cause for concern that the two youngest daughters may exhibit acting out behavior either now or in the future? What should Beth do to try to prevent this from occurring?

Substance Abuse Program — Kenny

Kenny is a 17-year-old male whose disposition requirement includes successful completion of a county-operated substance abuse program. This particular program involves a 30-day residential stay at the beginning, followed by five months' attendance in weekly individual and group counseling sessions. Kenny is also required to successfully complete 18 months of juvenile probation to begin upon release from the residential portion of the substance abuse program.

Kenny came to the attention of the juvenile court system as a result of a police report sent to the juvenile probation office regarding a situation during which the police determined he was under the influence of inhalants. An anonymous caller had reported to the police that a youth was at the city park sniffing spray paint from a rag, and was acting in a bizarre manner. Upon arrival at the park, the officer easily located Kenny. He was standing on a picnic table singing loudly. Before the officer could reach him, Kenny lost his balance and fell off the table. Because the officer was unsure of injuries, he called for an ambulance. Kenny had been holding onto a can of spray paint in one hand and a rag in the other hand with spray paint soaking the rag. The officer noted that Kenny had smears of spray paint on his face, mainly around his nose and mouth. An examination at the hospital determined that Kenny suffered only minor bruising as a result of his fall but was under the influence of inhalants. From the ID Kenny carried, police were sent to the family home to notify a parent or custodial guardian. After several hours went by and the parent(s) were not located, Kenny was admitted to the hospital to be kept under 24-hour observation. He was released to the custody of the police the following day. An officer made contact with Kenny's mother after Kenny was in detention for three days. Numerous messages were left on the home phone and notes were posted on the front and back doors of the home to contact the police department immediately, but Kenny's mother never made contact with the police or the juvenile authorities. A neighbor told the police where the mother might be located, and an officer made contact with her at a local bar. When approached by the officer, who informed the mother that he needed to speak with her about her son, she replied that she "expected the day would come when someone told her that Kenny had killed himself." The officer's report notes that Kenny's mother was inebriated at the time he made contact with her.

Kenny has a history of truancy, incorrigibility (several reports made by the mother to the probation office), three offenses for minor-in-possession of alcohol, and running away from home on four prior occasions. Kenny's first recorded encounter with the local city police occurred when he was 12. School records show that Kenny stopped coming to school when he was in the tenth grade and 16 years old. Prior to that time Kenny had mainly failing grades, starting in the ninth grade with marginally passing grades prior to that.

When Kenny's mother did not attend any of the court proceedings, Kenny was formally made a ward of the court to legally place him in the residential substance abuse program. Charges of neglect are pending against Kenny's mother.

Sarah, a case manager employed with the county substance abuse program, is assigned to track Kenny's progress in the program and to develop an intervention plan for when he is released on probation. She recently received her Bachelor's degree in criminal justice from the local university and has been employed with the county for six months. After reviewing Kenny's extensive file of previous contacts with the probation office, Sarah is deeply concerned about this case for two main reasons. First, she is baffled why none of the prior contacts with the juvenile justice system resulted in planned intervention for Kenny, such as a follow up with Child Protective Services, a school representative, or a disposition requiring probation. Second, she feels totally unqualified to provide Kenny the type of assistance he needs, based on the multitude of challenges he faces. She feels somewhat relieved that she has 30 days to develop a plan of intervention while Kenny is relatively safe in the residential substance abuse program.

Assignment 4.3

1. Do you think that Sarah should attempt to address her concerns that Kenny should have received attention from the juvenile justice system much earlier? Why or why not? Explain your answer.

2. Why do you think no prior formal intervention had been pursued in Kenny's case? Although your response will be opinion based, you need to support your position with information you have learned about the criminal justice system.

3. If you were in Sarah's position, what would you include in the intervention plan? Be sure to be thorough in your response and address the multitude of issues noted in the information presented.

4. Do you think that Sarah should assist Kenny in seeking emancipation? Why or why not? What would be the process if she decides to take this action? If you do not know what this means, research information about it.

5. What does the research indicate as the best intervention to use with youthful inhalant abusers? Does the research indicate that inhalant abuse often co-occurs with alcohol use?

6. Do you think the traditional 12-step program used by Alcoholics Anonymous is the appropriate approach to use with inhalant abusers? Why or why not? If you are not familiar with the AA program, research information about it.

7. Research the topic of inhalant abuse and write a brief paper (approximately three pages), summarizing the information. Pay particular attention to information about frequency of use among teenage populations and co-occurrence with alcohol and/or illegal drug use.

8. Do you feel that Kenny's mother should be prosecuted for neglect? Explain the rationale for your answer. If your answer is yes, what should be the consequence if she is convicted?

9. Why will Kenny continue under the supervision of the juvenile probation office after he turns age 18? What is the maximum age that the juvenile criminal justice system can maintain supervision over a youthful offender?

10. Based on the information presented in this case study, is Kenny likely to be an adult offender? If your answer is yes, what offense(s) do you think he may commit? If your answer is no, what do you think are the pivotal factor(s) that may contribute to Kenny's lack of criminal involvement?

Juvenile Detention Facility — Holly

Holly is a 14-year-old female currently housed in a county-operated juvenile detention facility. She was taken into custody by a city police officer who responded to report of a fight ensuing between a group of females in the parking lot of a local department store. A petition has been filed with the county probation office on charges of possession of a firearm (handgun) and aggravated assault. Witnesses at the scene of the altercation indicated that a physical fight had broken out between a group of approximately 14 teenaged females after an extended period of heated verbal exchange. Information indicates that Holly was thrown to the ground by two females who kicked her in various locations, including her stomach and head, at which point Holly pulled a handgun from her backpack and aimed it at both the girls who were kicking her, screaming repeatedly, "Now you will die. I will kill you." Witnesses state that the girls involved ran in various directions when they heard sirens. Holly and two others were lying on the ground when the officers arrived. All three were transported to the local hospital. Holly was taken to the detention center after being released that same evening from the hospital. A search of her backpack revealed the gun. While Holly was treated at the hospital for bruises and cuts, the parents of two females apparently involved in the altercation made a complaint to the police of an assault on their daughters by a female who threatened to kill them with a gun.

Holly has been at the detention facility for 72 hours. During this time period police officers have ascertained that the altercation was the result of a dispute between members of two gangs. The investigation entailed obtaining statements from witnesses who were at the scene at the time of the altercation, school officials, and some of the girls involved in the fight. Juvenile probation office records indicate that three prior petitions had been filed with the office, one for truancy, one for bringing a weapon to school, which resulted in expulsion, and one for incorrigibility, filed by Holly's mother.

Holly is a freshman at an alternative high school. School records indicate that Holly has been regularly attending school, earned passing grades in all six of her classes, and maintained good behaviors since beginning of school three months prior. Her teachers indicate that she is a quiet student who appears to adjust to new friends. Three teachers expressed concern that they had heard rumors that she was being recruited to join a local all female gang, but they did not note anything to indicate that she had done so.

George is a juvenile probation officer who has been assigned to complete a predisposition report for the juvenile court. After reading all of the police and school reports both from Holly's previous school and her current one, he interviews Holly's mother and discovers that she had filed the incorrigibility report with the probation office when Holly ran away from home after an argument over Holly's choice in boyfriends. Her mother, Krista, tells George that she became more and more concerned over Holly's change in behavior after she started seeing a 17 year old whom she met when she started high school at her previous school. At this time Holly frequently broke curfew and Krista noted the smell of alcohol when Holly came home. Krista works at a local restaurant from 4:00 p.m. to midnight or later, five to seven days a week. An only child, Holly's parents divorced one year earlier. Her father moved across the country, remarried, and maintains no contact with Holly or her mother. Krista tells George that she started her job due to financial difficulties and that she had not worked out of the home prior to the separation and divorce. She explains that she would much prefer a job that would allow her to be at home when Holly is out of school. Although she applied for various positions, the only employment opportunity she found was in food service. She hopes that after gaining more experience she will become employed at another restaurant that can offer her daytime work hours.

Assignment 4.4

1. Make a list of all of the factors that are likely to have contributed to Holly's current behavior. Which of the factors from the list do you think the juvenile court system could have a positive impact on? Explain your answer in detail.

2. What recommendation do you think George should make to the juvenile court judge in reference to disposition of Holly's case? Explain the rationale for the recommendation and cite information from the case.

3. Is a charge of aggravated assault appropriate, based on the circumstances of the case? Why or why not? Explain in detail using information from the case.

4. If the judge decides to require Holly to be supervised by the juvenile probation office, what should the intervention plan include?

5. If the judge decides that Holly should be placed in a state-operated juvenile correctional facility, what should be included in the case management plan?

6. Should George try to assist Krista, Holly's mother, in finding alternative employment that would allow her to be home with Holly after school hours? Address specifically whether juvenile court employees should provide intervention services to family members of a juvenile.

7. Do you think that Holly should be allowed to continue as a student in the alternative high school if she is placed on juvenile pro-

bation? In your response include both the positive and negative consequences one could expect if Holly continues in the alternative high school.

8. Should the criminal justice system pursue an investigation of Holly's 17-year-old boyfriend? Explain your answer.

Correctional Placement — Gary

Gary is a 16-year-old male currently placed in a state-operated juvenile correctional facility. Housed in the juvenile facility since he was 14 years old on multiple counts of child sexual molestation, he will continue to be under residential correctional placement until he turns 21. The disposition Gary received resulted from an agreement between Gary's attorney and the state prosecutor that Gary would not be charged as an adult offender, and in return he would be incarcerated until the age of 21. For the entire time he has been incarcerated, Gary has been housed in a maximum security facility in a unit designated specifically for sexual offenders.

The summary of the offenses leading to the disposition indicates that Gary sexually molested seven females ranging in age from six to nine over a period of two years. The victims lived in the same neighborhood as Gary and his family. Witness statements included in police reports and court documents indicate that Gary initiated friendships with the girls, first by giving them candy, then trinkets, then various items the girls had told him they wanted, such as toys, in one case a Barbie doll, and electronics, such as video games. The offenses were discovered after two of the girls were overheard by a parent arguing over what Gary had given one of the girls as a "reward" for what she did for him. Statements from the girls indicated that Gary asked them to touch "his privates" and allow him to "pet them in the privates."

Before incarceration, Gary lived with his biological mother and father in an up-scale suburban neighborhood. He is an only child. Both parents work in banking and financial investments. After years of trying to have children, they conceived Gary when they were both in their mid-forties. Gary's mother stopped working for two years, then resumed her job, leaving Gary to be cared for by various in-home child care providers.

Gary is required to attend individual counseling sessions once a week and participate in a group treatment program that meets twice a week. Although Gary has been in compliance with these requirements, the case file notes indicate that he seldom volunteers information, never of a personal nature, and answers questions only with monosyllable responses. He avoids joining others in group recreational activities. If a situation arises where he might be a part of a group activity, Gary has stated he is sick to his stomach or has a severe headache and asks to be allowed to stay in his living quarters or to be seen at the infirmary. Although numerous medical tests have been completed, none show a physical basis for his illnesses. No disciplinary reports have been filed during Gary's incarceration.

Gary spends a great deal of time reading and drawing. He uses money from his account established by his parents to purchase art supplies. He has continued his education and is scheduled to take his GED in six months. A community volunteer that comes to the facility to teach art classes told Lisa, his case manager, that he feels Gary has the potential to be accepted into an art program for continued instruction upon release from the facility.

Lisa has been Gary's case manager since his arrival at the facility. Although she strongly suspects that Gary himself was the victim of child molestation, she has no evidence or statements from Gary to confirm her suspicion, since nothing in his file gives conclusive information that Gary was abused. However, Lisa's 18 years of work in the correctional facility, including seven years with sexual offenders, makes her feel strongly that Gary was a victim as a young child.

Throughout the past two years, Gary's parents have retained an attorney to appeal his disposition and petition for a reduction in the length of his sentence. The state court of appeals recently agreed to rule on the appeal. In response to the attorney's request that Gary's case manager provide a detailed report of his progress toward "rehabilitation," the court has ordered the report be completed and include an evaluation of Gary's future dangerousness to society.

Assignment 4.5

1. Do you think that Gary's lack of participation in group activities reflects negatively on his progress toward rehabilitation? Why or why not? Explain your answer using information from the case study.

2. If you were Gary's case manager, what would you do to get Gary to engage in group activities? Be detailed in your answer, describing the activities and your method to get him more involved.

3. If you were on a debate team that takes the position that Gary should not be released from the facility anytime short of his 21st birthday, how would you argue your position?

4. If you were on a debate team that takes the position that the length of time of the disposition should be reviewed with the possibility for early release from incarceration, what would be your rationale?

5. Locate three professional research studies that examine the topic of recidivism of juvenile sexual offenders. Summarize the studies including the sample size, the data collection methods, the data analysis methods, and the conclusions. Do the studies you used for this exercise support the appeal for early release or the original length of disposition?

6. Are special programs for juvenile sex offenders available in the area where you live? Contact a representative of an institutional or community-based program, and determine what interventions it uses to deter recidivism.

7. Based on the information in this case, does Gary present a high, medium, or low risk for future danger to society? Explain you answer.

Aftercare Services—Marti

Marti is a 17-year-old female who will be released soon from a juvenile correctional facility after being incarcerated for nine months as the result of a disposition for child endangerment. A summary of the offense report indicates that police were dispatched to an apartment complex where they located Marti and her boyfriend inebriated and asleep while a six-month-old male child was crying loudly in another room. Child protective services responded at the request of the police and took the child into protective custody. A medical examination by a pediatrician determined that the child was undernourished and underweight for his age. He had diaper burn with infected open sores, commonly the result of being kept in soiled diapers. He also had a severe inner ear infection in both ears, head lice, and an infection on his left arm, possibly the result of untreated insect bites.

Marti gave birth to her son when she was 16. She stated in a pre-sentence report that she does not know who the biological father of the child is. Prior to incarceration, Marti lived in a group home as a ward of the state. Her biological mother relinquished parental rights when Marti was 11 years old. At that time Marti's mother was sentenced to four years in prison on a conviction for trafficking in a controlled substance. According to the records, Marti's biological father is unknown. Throughout Marti's first 11 years, she lived with her mother the majority of the time but occasionally resided with a maternal aunt when her mother was in jail for alcohol and drug related violations.

Prior to being incarcerated, Marti attended an alternative high school, and completed ninth grade. She has continued to attend classes while at the correctional facility but is not prepared to take the GED. She has been diagnosed as having a mild intellectual disability, with an IQ of 61. Marti has completed a 16-week parenting education course at the facility and intends to petition for custody of her son upon release. She will turn 18 two months after her scheduled release date. Her case manager at the facility has recommended that her assigned aftercare officer explore the possibility of semi-independent living arrangements for Marti. Child protective services arranged for visits between Marti and her son at the facility once a month during her incarceration. Marti's son has been residing in a foster home since the night that Marti was taken into custody. Now fifteen months old, he has gained the appropriate weight, and is clear of all infections. It was determined by a physician that tubes in his ears were needed to aid in clearing the infection.

Blake, Marti's parole officer, has a caseload predominately consisting of adult parolees. In the office where Blake works, the common practice is to assign juvenile aftercare cases to the newest parole officer hired. This is the first professional position that Blake has had after receiving his Bachelor's degree in criminal justice eighteen months ago from the local university. He has seven other juvenile aftercare cases on his caseload, all males. After reviewing Marti's case file, Blake feels somewhat unprepared to address the issues involved in her case. In two weeks Marti will be released and will be required to participate in aftercare services until she is 21, potentially being under the supervision of the regional parole office for a little more than three years.

Assignment 4.6

1. Make a list of what Blake should do to prepare for Marti's release from the facility in two weeks. Be as detailed as possible and prioritize the list, based on what you think is most important to do first. Explain your reasoning for the actions you have included on the list you created.

2. Do you think that Marti should be allowed to take custody of her son? Explain your answer.

3. Do you think that the court is likely to allow Marti to gain custody of her son? Explain your answer, being sure to indicate the rationale for why you think the court will make such a decision.

4. Research a program that provides semi-independent living for young adults with developmental delays. Based on the description of the program, do you think Marti can benefit from such living arrangements? Explain your answer.

5. Is the practice the local parole office uses in assigning juvenile aftercare cases to the newest parole officer appropriate and effective? If you agree with this practice, explain why. If you disagree, explain why and describe what you think is a more effective assignment of cases.

6. What is the difference between child abuse and child neglect?

7. Research the number of reported child abuse and neglect cases in your county for the previous year. What is the number of reported cases? What is the number of substantiated cases? What is the source of this information?

8. Determine the national number of deaths of children under two that occurred in the previous year as a result of child abuse and/or neglect. What initiatives can you propose to lower this number?

Chapter Five

Correctional Administration

Introduction

The focus of this chapter is on a variety of issues that correctional administrators may encounter in providing services to offender populations. After each case study a list of questions is provided to serve as discussion points, homework assignments, topics for individual or group in- or out-of-class activities, and quiz and/or test subject matter. The objective of the questions is to encourage the reader to reflect on the variety of issues presented in the facts of each case. The reader is encouraged to consider thoroughly the issues presented and apply information learned in courses, knowledge of the criminal justice system (such as through employment and awareness of current events), review of research, and personal awareness, where appropriate. The cases portrayed in this chapter pertain to various situations that correctional administrators may encounter. This chapter focuses on six very different situations: (1) dealing with budgetary constraints, (2) adjusting caseloads, (3) providing inmate programs, (4) human resources management, (5) addressing litigation, and (6) gaining and maintaining accreditation.

Case Studies

Budgetary Constraints

Lawrence is an assistant superintendent of a medium security adult male prison with a rated capacity of 800 but currently housing 950 inmates. He has worked for the state Department of Correction (hereinafter abbreviated DOC) for 16 years. Lawrence has a Bachelor's degree in criminal justice and a Master's degree in counseling.

Lawrence worked his way up through the ranks, starting as a case manager in a disciplinary segregation cell block for six years. He applied for advancement and was promoted to supervisor of all case management at the facility, a position he held for eight years, when he was promoted into his current position as assistant superintendent. He did not apply for this position but, instead, was asked to work in this capacity after the firing of the previous assistant superintendent as the result of poor job performance reviews.

Lawrence has many job responsibilities including overseeing the revenues and expenditures for the facility. His other duties include serving on numerous facility committees, including disciplinary, mediation (dealing with lawsuits filed), and selection committees for new employees. He reports directly to the superintendent of the facility who has been in his position for only three years, having been appointed by the commissioner of corrections, who is also relatively new to her job, coming into the position after the election of a new governor for the state only three years earlier. The facility superintendent has no prior adult department of correction work experience. He previously worked as a top administrator for a private for profit mental health facility.

Lawrence directly supervises each of the seven cell block case managers, the director of mental health services, the director of recreational services, and all shift captains of the correctional officers. He also directly supervises the comptroller who manages the facility budget.

Due primarily to economic strains across the nation, the state department of correction has been instructed by the governor's office to cut the proposed budget for the upcoming fiscal year by 7%. The DOC Commissioner has directed all facilities in the state to submit a draft budget that reflects the 7% reduction. For the upcoming year, each facility must maintain the same number of inmates it housed the previous year. In other words, budget cuts cannot be based on a reduction in inmate numbers. Furthermore, a hiring freeze has been placed on all current DOC vacancies and any new vacancies that may occur in the next 12 months from resignations, terminations, or retirements.

Lawrence feels a great deal of pressure to comply with the Commissioner's directive. The superintendent tells Lawrence that he is really counting on him and his experience as a DOC employee, as well as his sixteen years working in the same facility. He also tells Lawrence that although he will review the draft budget proposal before it is sent to the Commissioner, he does not feel confident to assist in the development of the budget. The bottom line is that Lawrence and the comptroller are the two persons responsible for accomplishing the assigned task.

Assignment 5.1

1. Make a list of all the operating costs that compile a prison facility budget. You don't have to assign dollar amounts to the categories on the list. Just make the list by brainstorming on everything you can think to include.

2. Using the internet, research a budget for an adult medium security facility that houses approximately 1000 inmates.

3. Compare the list you created in your response to assignment #1 with what you found in response to assignment #2. What operating costs did you fail to include on your list that were included in the budget you researched? Do you have anything on your list that was not included in the researched budget?

4. Create a final list of categories to include in an operating budget for an adult male medium security facility that houses approximately 1000 inmates. Again, you do not need to designate any dollar amounts to the categories. The goal of this exercise is to compare your answers to #1 and #2 above to create a comprehensive, realistic list of operating costs.

5. Designate a percent of the total budget to assign to each category on the list you developed through your response to assignment #4. The information you researched from assignment #2 above should guide you in approximating the percent of a budget to des-

ignate for each category. For example, you might decide that personnel costs would be 67% of the total budget, health care services 3%, food services 4%, and so on.

6. Using your responses to assignments #4 and #5, state how you would decrease the overall operating costs by 7%. Provide an explanation and a justification for your proposed reductions. For example, if you decide that the reduction of 7% in operating costs would come in combination of a 4% cut in personnel costs and the other 3% through reductions in health services, explain what the specific reductions in the budget for these categories would be, and justify why you think your allocation is the best way to reduce costs.

7. What consequences might result from the budget reductions you suggest in response to assignment #6?

8. Do you think that Lawrence is overcommitted in job responsibilities? If yes, what do you suggest to reduce his work load so that he can concentrate his efforts on budgetary issues?

9. Do you think that Lawrence's education and work experience prepared him for his current work responsibilities? If yes, what from his background prepared him for his current duties? If no, in what areas do you think he lacks education or work experience, and what do you suggest to overcome this deficit?

10. Do you think that anyone who is politically appointed to be a superintendent of a department of corrections facility should be required to have education and/or work experience in corrections? Why or why not? Include your thoughts on the advantages of having education and/or work experience in corrections. What other education or work experience may qualify someone for such a position?

Adjusting Caseloads

Bonnie is the Chief Adult Probation Officer with a current office caseload population of 4,000 clients; 2,800 are on probation for a Class A misdemeanor conviction and the remaining 1,200 were convicted of felonies ranging from Class A (most serious) to

Class D (least serious). Class A Misdemeanors include shoplifting, issuing worthless checks under $250, and criminal trespass. Class A felonies include aggravated rape, aggravated battery, aggravated robbery, and murder. Class B felonies include possession of narcotics, dealing in methamphetamines, carjacking, burglary, and child molestation. Class C felonies include possession of child pornography, receiving stolen property, auto theft, and identity deception. Class D felonies include possession of marijuana, battery, resisting arrest, and forgery. The class of felony for violent crimes depends on whether a weapon was involved and/or bodily injury occurred. In the case of drug offenses, the class depends on the type and amount of drug and, if dealing, the place where the offense occurred. The class of felony for white collar crimes depends significantly on the amount of money involved. Of the total felony caseload, 80 are Class A offenders, 160 are Class B offenders, 310 are Class C offenders, and 650 are Class D offenders.

Bonnie supervises 20 probation officers of whom four are in their first year of employment and are considered to be probationary status. The remaining 16 officers have varying years of experience, ranging from three to 22 years. Bonnie has 27 years experience as a probation officer and has been the Chief for the past six years.

Three years earlier the county probation office had 24 officer positions, but budget reductions in the county budget forced a hiring freeze. Consequently, many of the officers experienced an increase in their caseloads as the clients of four officers who vacated their positions had to be divided amongst the remaining 20 officers. Ten of the officers supervise misdemeanor clients and ten supervise felony clients, with caseloads equally divided amongst the officers. Those supervising misdemeanor clients have caseloads of 280 each and those supervising felony clients have caseloads of 120 each. All officers write presentencing reports, ordered for felony clients, on a rotation basis. The office averages 400 reports a year.

Bonnie has a Master's degree in counseling. All probation officers are required to have a Bachelor's degree in a social service area. Sixteen of the officers have a Bachelor's degree in criminal justice, sociology, or psychology, two of the officers have a Master's degree in social work, one of the officers has both Bachelor's and Master's degree in education, and one of the officers has a Master's degree in business administration with a Bachelor's degree in general studies.

Recently, the majority of the officers have met with Bonnie individually to express their dissatisfaction with the job, mainly due to caseload size and their inability to provide required services to the clients, whether it be surveillance or intervention, because of a lack of time. Several of them expressed the concern that they believe many of the clients are violating conditions of their probation and engaging in criminal activity because the clients know that the officers are overwhelmed with too many clients and not enough time.

Bonnie has also received complaints from the district court judges, who are dissatisfied with the level of surveillance provided by the officers, the increasing number of probation violation reports being submitted, and the failure of the officers to meet deadlines for presentencing reports, causing delays in sentencing.

In talking with other chief probation officers around the state, Bonnie discovers that all large county offices are experiencing the same types of challenges. After conducting some research, she finds that some states have implemented a variety of strategies to deal with similar circumstances. She is considering several options, such as:

- Specialized caseloads based on class of felony: Officers supervising Felony Class A and B clients have reduced caseloads.
- Specialized caseloads based on type of crime: For example, all sex offenders are assigned to one officer, all firearms offenders are assigned to another officer, all burglary offenders are assigned to several officers, etc.
- One officer, who has no caseload, writes all presentence reports.
- Supervise only clients with felony convictions and, with judicial agreement, misdemeanor clients are placed on non-reporting or mail-in status.
- Division of labor for officers: One group of officers is assigned to surveillance, including monitoring for restitution and community service, another group of officers monitors services, assisting clients with referrals to service providers in the area.

This strategy allows clients to have regular contact with several officers.

Assignment 5.2

1. Treating the five strategies Bonnie is considering as separate options, rank order them from most desirable to least desirable, listing the best first.

2. Which option(s) above do you think would be most agreeable to the majority of the officers? Explain and justify your answer, based on information from the case.

3. Which option(s) outlined above do you think would best address the officers' main concern of caseload size? Explain your answer, using information from the case.

4. Which options outlined above do you think would best address the concerns of the judges? Explain your answer, using information from the case.

5. If Bonnie chose to use specialized caseloads, which of the two options stated above do you think would be the better choice? Explain your answer.

6. How could clients benefit from having multiple officers interacting with each client and having some officers in charge of surveillance and other officers in charge of intervention services?

7. What could be potential difficulties in managing client cases if multiple officers interact with each client and some officers are responsible for surveillance while others are responsible for intervention services?

8. Should Bonnie take into consideration the educational qualifications of officers in assigning caseloads? If yes, how should caseloads be divided based on this criterion? If no, explain why not?

9. If you were seeking employment as a probation officer, which option(s) would you prefer? Explain your answer.

10. What other strategies might Bonnie consider in addressing the concerns of the officers?

11. What other strategies might Bonnie consider in addressing the concerns of the judges?

12. Which strategy(ies) do you think would be the most effective in decreasing client recidivism? Explain your answer.

13. What negative consequences might result from putting misdemeanor clients on non-reporting or mail-in status? What are possible benefits?

14. What do you think is the ideal caseload size for officers supervising Class A and B felony offenders? Explain your answer.

15. What do you think is the ideal caseload size for officers supervising Class C and D felony offenders? Explain your answer.

16. Do you think that the four officers on probationary employment status should supervise Class A and B felony offenders? Why or why not?

Provision of Inmate Programs

Carter is the superintendent of a maximum security adult male correctional facility. The facility, which currently houses 800 inmates, has a rated bed capacity of 780. Eighty-two percent of the inmates are incarcerated for a violent crime, specifically forcible rape (including 56 inmates convicted of crimes involving children), second or first degree murder, armed robbery, and aggravated assault. The remaining 18% of the population are inmates who, due to their assaultive behavior toward other inmates and correctional staff when housed in a lower security level facility, are now housed in the maximum security facility. The average sentence of current inmates is 47 years. A few of the inmates will most likely never be released due to the length of their sentence, some 200 and 300 years, unless an appeal results in a reduced sentence or release. However, the vast majority of the inmates will be released back into society. Inmates are awarded one day good time for every day served in prison. Consequently, the majority of the inmates will be released in a little over 20 years.

Carter has been employed in corrections for 28 years. He started as a case manager in a medium security facility, where he remained for eight years. He was promoted to a supervisory position in charge of all the case managers at the maximum security facility, where he currently works, a position he held for seven years. He was next promoted to the assistant superintendent position and worked in this role for five years. He has been superintendent of the facility for eight years. Carter had a Bachelor's degree in sociology when he was first hired as a case manager and earned a Master's degree in public administration ten years ago.

The closer Carter gets to retiring in another two years, the more he finds himself reflecting on how much corrections operations have changed through the almost three decades he has worked at the facility. He has seen the pendulum shift back and forth from a focus on containment and control to a focus on inmate services to assist in the re-entry of the inmate back to society. In previous years he has always been comfortable with making adjustments to changes, which most often occurred with the election of a new governor who appointed his/her preferred commissioner. However, he now finds himself facing a dilemma as he is confronted daily with decisions that must be made to continue or eliminate inmate programs due to a lack of funding. The State has a $157 million dollar deficit and Carter has been ordered by the Commissioner to reduce the annual operating expenses currently allocated for prison programs by 12% for the upcoming annual budget reviews.

Carter is also fully aware of the negative opinions of some of the correctional officers who criticize inmate programs and, the more recent outcry from various factions in the community, that taxpayer dollars are being used unwisely for these programs. Correctional officers, in general, have expressed the least favorable opinion toward the counseling programs but are supportive of recreation and job training programs. In contrast, a particularly vocal community group is displeased with recreational programs, particularly that weightlifting equipment is allowed for inmates, especially violent offenders housed in a maximum security facility. Also a large union represented in the community disapproves of the facility's program to provide job training in a skilled trade because released inmates will then compete for job opportunities. A group of local university students and some parents have started to lobby against providing educational programs, specifically college courses for inmates at taxpayer expense, while many of them are struggling to pay for their own education or that of their children. Yet another community group has complained to the governor's office that too much money is spent on counseling programs. They cite numerous research articles that conclude that involvement in counseling does not reduce recidivism.

Carter is taking all of these views into consideration and weighing whether the opinions expressed are valid. In addition, Carter asked his assistant superintendent to compile a report, that lists all inmate programs and percent of total program costs each represents. The following summarizes the information he will use to make decisions on lowering the costs by 12%:

Education Programs: Costs include a portion of the program director's salary, wages for part-time instructors of education programs and classes, and materials for courses   28%

Vocational Programs: Costs include a portion of the program director's salary, wages for part-time job training personnel, and materials and supplies   35%

Recreation Programs: Costs include a portion of the program director's salary. The major portion of money allocated supports weightlifting apparatus and upkeep of the gymnasium.   17%

Counseling Programs: Costs include the salary for one full-time psychologist, one part-time substance abuse counselor, one part-time social worker, and supplies, such as workbooks for inmates   8%

Pre-release Program: Costs include a portion of the program director's salary, part-time salary for a case manager who is also responsible for re-entry planning, and materials, such as workbooks   8%

Miscellaneous Programs: Remaining costs are
allocated to a variety of programs, mainly for
supplies and materials such as for art programs,
religious programs, and Alcoholics and Narcotics
Anonymous   4%

Assignment 5.3

1. What adjustments to the allocated percents should Carter make?
Explain your answer and justify your suggestions for reducing costs,
not just the percents, but how savings can be made.

2. If you were involved in a debate about the benefits of having a
recreational program available for inmates at this facility, including the weightlifting equipment, what information would you present to convince others to approve the continuation of the program?
If you opposed the program, what information would you present
to convince others to disapprove continuation of the program?

3. If you were involved in a debate about the benefits of continuing the counseling programs for inmates at this facility, what information would you use to support continuation of the program?
Take the other side of the issue: what information would you present to convince others to disapprove continuation of the program?

4. If Carter's only option is to eliminate one or more of the programs
described in the report, which program(s) should he eliminate?
Explain your answer.

5. Should any program described in the report not receive a reduction of funding? Explain your answer.

6. Does the community group opposed to job training programs
have a valid argument? Explain your answer.

7. During incarceration should inmates have access to earning a
college degree for free or a reduced cost? Explain the reasoning for
your position. Is your answer the same for inmates that, in all likelihood, will never return to the community, based on their length

of sentence? Should they be given an option of higher education? Explain your answer.

8. Why do you think the correctional officers at this facility are, in general, opposed to counseling programs? Do you think their objection to these programs is the same or different from the reason the community group opposes the counseling programs? Explain your answer.

9. Do you think any and every religious preference should be allowable in a correctional facility? Why or why not? Explain and justify your answer.

10. Do you think that the type and number of programs available for inmates should vary based on security level of the facility? Explain your answer.

Personnel Issues

Donna has recently been hired by the state department of corrections as human resources manager, a newly created position, in a juvenile facility that houses 550 youth. She has replaced a woman, Violet, who retired after 30 years working at the same facility. Violet started at the facility as a secretary to the assistant superintendent. Her position title later changed to administrative assistant when the department of corrections reviewed all job descriptions under a civil suit filed by the employees' union. She later became the administrative assistant to the new superintendent when his predecessor transferred to an adult facility. The new superintendent, who wanted someone with extensive experience working with administrators at the facility, had Violet's job description changed to include management of recruitment, selection, and promotion of facility employees.

Donna is a recent graduate with a Bachelor's degree in business administration. During college, she had one course focused specifically on human resources management. Donna's father and two uncles work in the state department of corrections in management positions in the Commissioner's office. By serving as personal references, they were instrumental in helping Donna get her job.

Donna is somewhat concerned that her co-workers may not approve of the way she got her job, but she sincerely hopes that her job performance will prove that she deserves her position.

The superintendent tells Donna that he wants her to become familiar with all job descriptions and policies and procedures used for recruitment, selection, and promotion. Next he wants her to review personnel files to make sure that all policies and procedures were followed and that the records accurately reflect that personnel meet the requirements for the positions they hold, based on the job description of required education and experience. She must also check the personnel files to verify that personnel have met annual training requirements, if applicable.

Donna quickly sees that policies and procedures issued from the central office on recruitment, selection, and promotion are detailed and understandable. However, the job descriptions appear outdated, the majority of personnel records are incomplete, and participation in required training is not documented. After bringing the situation to the superintendent's attention, he tells her to talk with the various supervisors and ask them to assist in completing personnel files with all needed documentation and updating the job descriptions. To save time and not have to repeat her request, Donna decides that the best approach is to call a group meeting to explain to all the supervisors what she needs. She sets a date and time and sends out a memo two weeks prior to the scheduled meeting. When the date arrives, only three supervisors, less than 10%, attend the meeting. Perplexed, she decides that maybe people just didn't have time to meet, so she composes a detailed memo to explain what she needs and asks supervisors to provide the information for all personnel they oversee. She asks that everything be given to her in two weeks. As the date comes and goes, she still does not get responses from the supervisors. Somewhat frustrated, she decides to talk with each supervisor individually. She is repeatedly told the same thing: "Violet never asked us for this information," "Violet didn't need our help; she was able to do the job herself," and "Violet appreciated the fact that we are all busy people." Donna's supervisor recently asked her for an update on her review of the personnel records and making sure that all are in order for an upcoming accreditation review. She feels defeated and stressed to the point of turning in her resignation after only six months on the job.

Assignment 5.4

1. Why do you think the supervisors may be resistant to fulfilling Donna's requests for information? Identify the reasons, using information from the case study. From this list, what do you think is the number one reason why she is not getting the cooperation she needs from the supervisors?

2. If you were in a human resources management position and given the same task as Donna to update the personnel files, how would you approach completing the task? Be detailed in your answer.

3. What process would you use to update the job descriptions? Who should information come from to get this task completed? Explain your answer.

4. Donna is experiencing a common challenge that occurs when a new employee takes on many of the job responsibilities of a person who has been in the position for a number of years. What suggestions would you make to Donna to help her gain the respect of other correctional employees? How should she respond to references made to the way things were done in the past?

5. Based on the information in the case, should Donna have been hired for this position? Why or why not? Use information from the case to justify your response.

6. If you were developing a policy to establish the process for promotion of correctional officers to supervisory positions, what weight would you assign seniority and higher education? Explain your answer.

7. What information should be included in every job description? Create a "boilerplate" job description depicting the categories of information that should be included.

8. Locate and print job descriptions for five separate types of positions in corrections facility employment in the state in which you live. Do the job descriptions you located include all of the information you expected to find? What was not included that you think should be?

9. Do you think that corrections department employees should be required to complete a minimum of 40 hours of continuing education units (training) annually? Why or why not? If you think they should, what type of continuing education would be the most beneficial? Explain your answer.

10. What methods should a corrections department use to recruit qualified candidates for corrections employment?

11. What steps should be included in the selection process for corrections officer positions? Rank these steps in importance and justify your answer.

12. What should be the educational requirements for each one of the following corrections department positions? Explain your response for each.

1. Corrections officer
2. Corrections officer supervisor
3. Case manager
4. Corrections counselor
5. Assistant superintendent
6. Facility superintendent

Legal Issues

Benjamin is a court appointed compliance coordinator for a maximum security adult male corrections facility. His educational qualifications for this position are that he has a Master's degree in Public Administration and a Jurist Doctorate Degree. However, he does not have any prior work experience in corrections. He was previously a public defender for eight years in a large county office. He has been in the position as compliance coordinator for the state Department of Corrections for the previous three months.

The facility where Benjamin works operates under a consent decree, per an agreement reached between the state-operated corrections facility and the federal court seven years earlier. A lawsuit had been filed by the inmates under Section 1983 of the Civil Rights Act 11 years earlier. The suit claimed that facility conditions violated Eighth Amendment protection from cruel and unusual punishment, specifically pertaining to the following conditions:

(1) Lack of adequate heating, venting, and air-conditioning in the cell blocks, leading to life endangerment
(2) Lack of adequate nutrition in food provided, leading to increased risk of physical illnesses
(3) Invasion of privacy, leading to psychological trauma as a result of female corrections officers supervising shower activities of male inmates
(4) Extended periods of lockdown, resulting in psychological trauma and recurrent physical ailments
(5) Failure to provide a safe environment, resulting in psychological trauma, physical injury, and death
(6) Overcrowded conditions leading to an unsafe living environment and unsanitary conditions, such as overflowing sewer backing up through drains in shower areas, resulting in increased risk of infectious diseases

Built in the early 1900s, the facility, the oldest in the state and the only one rated as maximum security, has had few modifications over more than 100 years. The rated capacity is 2200, but it currently houses approximately 2850 inmates. It has constantly been understaffed over the past 15 years, with an annual turnover rate of 38% of officers. Many officers work 12- and 16-hour shifts to compensate for the shortage in staff. The correctional officers' union has recently filed a complaint with the superintendent's office, based on the risk to safety resulting from the shortage in officers.

A primary responsibility of the compliance coordinator, Benjamin, is to report quarterly to the federal court reference all actions taken by the corrections department to address the six issues cited in the inmates' lawsuit. The court stipulated that the facility is to demonstrate "reasonable progress" towards rectifying the causes of the complaints addressed in the lawsuit. A time limit was not a part of the consent decree, but the court did stipulate that if "reasonable progress" was not being made, the corrections department could be fined $5,000 a day for not being in compliance with the consent decree.

The superintendent of the facility instructed Benjamin to submit an initial plan to address the issues set forth in the lawsuit within 30 days of his hiring. He must also submit monthly reports to the superintendent detailing actions taken to comply with the plan. These monthly reports will form the basis for the quarterly reports required by the federal court. As such, they must be detailed and accurate.

Assignment 5.5

1. What do you think the court means and expects by "reasonable progress"? In your response, create a definition of this term that includes a means to measure whether this expectation is being met.

2. What should Benjamin include in the initial plan? This plan should include actions to show "reasonable progress" in addressing each of the inmates' six complaints separately. Be sure to be detailed in your response but also realistic, taking into consideration budget deficits in the Department of Corrections.

3. Do you think that Benjamin should get input from other Department of Corrections employees in developing the initial plan? If so, who should he consult and why? If not, explain.

4. Rank the list of complaints from the simplest to the most difficult to address, with "1" being the simplest and "6" being the most difficult. Provide a rationale for your ranking.

5. Complaints filed by both the inmates and the officers' union share a commonality. What is the common complaint? In what ways could the inmates and the officers work together to address this complaint?

6. Which one of the six complaints filed by the inmates is the likely causal factor of a number of the other complaints? Create a computer graphic that illustrates how these complaints are related.

7. Develop a computer-generated timeline that projects when actions included in the plan should be initiated and shows benchmarks illustrative of "reasonable progress."

8. What would you suggest to the superintendent to assist him in addressing the correctional officers' union complaint of safety risk as a result of understaffed conditions? In your response, be sure to include detail about how to reduce the 38% turnover, keeping in mind the budget deficits in the state.

9. Should corrections officers be allowed to work 16-hour shifts? Why or why not?

Accreditation

Catherine is an Assistant Superintendent at a medium security women's corrections facility. She has been given the directive by the superintendent that she is to manage the process involved in seeking accreditation of the facility through the American Correctional Association. The facility has been pursuing accreditation over the past several years, with the first external site review team visit five years earlier and the most recent six months ago. The recent report developed by the consultants that conducted the standards compliance audit cited the following deficiencies which kept the facility from being accredited:

1. Safety: ratio of officer to inmate
   The audit confirmed that in the 12 months prior to the audit, there were numerous times that only 10 correctional officers were on shift to monitor the activities of 750 inmates.

2. Care: availability of medical services
   During the audit, inmate complaints about the lack of medical services were carefully reviewed. It was determined that on numerous occasions, medical services were not provided in a manner appropriate to the seriousness of the medical need. A lack of the available medical services resulted in three wrongful death lawsuits in the 12 months prior to the audit, which the inmates' families won.

Catherine has been in the position of Assistant Superintendent for only six months. She began her career in corrections as an officer at the same facility and was in this position for six years. During this time she attended courses at the local university, earned a Bachelor's degree in administration, with a minor in criminal justice. After receiving her degree she moved into the position of case manager, which she worked for eight years. She later was promoted to be the Director of Prison Programs, a position she held for two years before being promoted to Assistant Superintendent. Although her experience in various employment roles has provided Catherine broad insight into the operations of a corrections facility, she is concerned that she may not be able to complete the work directive.

The Department of Corrections in the state in which Catherine is employed is experiencing budget cutbacks. The obvious way to correct the two cited deficiencies and meet the standards for accreditation is to increase the budget for the prison to hire more corrections officers and medical personnel. Catherine meets with the Superintendent to discuss the need for more funding to meet the standards. He tells her to develop a plan that includes an adjustment in the budget to save from other areas of prison operations, along with detail of needed increases in funding to rectify the cited deficits. He believes that this approach will indicate to the Commissioner of Corrections in the state that the facility is putting forth a good faith effort to develop a plan that does not merely ask for more money but, instead, demonstrates a strategy that includes adjusting the current line items in the budget to save costs.

Assignment 5.6

1. Research the accreditation standards of the American Correctional Association and determine the main areas that are audited during a site visit. Two of the areas are discussed in this case study, but there are other areas also audited.

2. Determine what is considered the optimal inmate-to-officer ratio for a medium security adult facility. Contact a facility in your state and determine what ratio they use.

3. Determine what is considered the optimal detainee-to-officer ratio for a state-operated juvenile facility. Why do you think there is often a difference in the optimal ratios of a juvenile and an adult facility?

4. Corrections facility reports frequently provide information about "inmate-to-corrections facility staff ratio." In scrutinizing safety risk factors to officers and inmates, why is it important to determine the officer-to-inmate ratio instead of the staff-to-inmate ratio?

5. Make a list of categories to be funded in operating a prison such as programs, building maintenance, food services, etc.

6. What prison operating costs may be trimmed to shift money to personnel costs to hire more officers and reduce the inmate-to-officer ratio? Explain your reasoning for why you think these operating costs can be reduced. What may be consequences from your proposed budget adjustments?

7. Brainstorm ways that adequate medical services can be provided for the least amount of additional funding. Think of creative options, even if they might be difficult to implement.

8. Whom should Catherine involve in group meetings to brainstorm possible solutions? Explain your rationale for those you suggest for inclusion.

9. Develop a timetable that depicts the main activities that need to occur to develop the plan that Catherine is directed to submit to the Superintendent. Use a computer graphic software program to develop the timetable.

10. Research the number of wrongful death lawsuits filed by inmates' families and/or activist groups over the past three years in the state where you live. Is this number higher or lower than you would expect? Explain your answer.

Chapter Six

Reports

Introduction

The focus of this chapter is on a number of common reports used in day-to-day correctional operations. The requirements of what to include in reports and how to structure them is likely to vary based on jurisdiction. Individual case circumstances and agency operating procedures will dictate what reports are required. However, the general content is likely to be common across jurisdictions. The main purpose of the reports is also discussed. The reader should be aware that many other reports are used in correctional operations other than those discussed in this chapter. As with preceding chapters, assignments are included after each report to provide the reader an opportunity to engage in critical thinking and to integrate learning. The chapter begins with an example of a presentence report. Using the information about the defendant in the presentence report, attention is next given to probation and parole violation reports, followed by an example of a case log including some suggestions for what type of information is commonly included and why and what type of information is usually not a part of a case log and why that is the case. This is followed with an example of a parole plan. The chapter ends with an example of a community corrections referral.

Presentence Report

Some agencies call this a PSR for presentencing report while other agencies term it a PSI for presentencing investigation. The purpose is the same regardless of title; to provide the sentencing judge with information about the offender and the offense that can be used in determining the appropriate sentence based on the individual case circumstance. It is important to remember that not all judges require a presentence report be compiled. Some judges order a presentence report but do not want the report to include any recommendation. Other judges order a presentence report and do want recommendations to be included.

The PSR is also used for case management, as it commonly contains information useful in determining the type of interventions needed to assist in preventing recidivism. Whether the person is placed on probation, sentenced to jail followed by probation, or sentenced to serve prison time followed by parole, officers, treatment workers, and education and vocation facilitators in the community and facilities can use the information in a PSR to plan and implement the most appropriate intervention.

The probation department is commonly responsible for completion of these reports. How the work is assigned, depends on the jurisdiction. Some probation offices have separate units whose sole responsibility is to complete the court-ordered presentence reports. Other offices rotate this assignment through the officers who also have the responsibility of caseload supervision. Some jurisdictions use a format requiring in-depth coverage of the various required components of the report. Others use an abbreviated format, that allows the respondent to indicate from among a variety of choices what is most appropriate to the individual case. In using this format the report is more a fill-in-the-blank/multiple-choice approach. An example of the longer, narrative version is provided here to give the reader an idea of the depth and breadth of the information commonly contained in these reports.

Example Presentence Report

Name:	John Doe	Date Interviewed: 01/20/10
AKA:	John Green	Docket#:
Address:	1500 Roosevelt St. Jonesboro, ___	Judge: Joseph Smith
Telephone:	None available	District Attorney: Simms

DOB:	01/01/82	Defense Attorney: Clark (public defender)
Age:	28	Probation Officer: Karl
Place of Birth:	Wellsville, Ohio	Scheduled Sentencing Date: 02/07/10
Race:	Caucasian	
Height:	5'11"	
Weight:	172 lbs.	
Hair:	Light brown	
Eyes:	Brown	
Dependents:	0	
Scars:	One-inch scar above right eyebrow; two-inch scar on inside of left forearm	
Tattoos:	Blue ink barbed wire encircling his neck and biceps of both arms	

Case Information

Date of Offense:	10/10/09	Arresting Agency: Westville Police Department
Charges:	Commercial Burglary—Section 34-27-16 of the Penal Code Felony C, punishable by a maximum of four years incarceration; Felony B, punishable by a maximum of 10 years incarceration if the burglary was of a pharmaceutical store or business; Felony A, punishable by 30 years if the defendant was in possession of a firearm or other deadly weapon at the time of the offense.	
Co-defendants:	None	
Date of Arrest:	10/10/09	Where Arrested: At _____ Drug Store
Total Days in Jail: 102		Detained/Bonded: Unable to post $25,000 bond

Summary of Offense Information:

Police reports indicate that the police responded to an alarm company report of a silent burglar alarm at a locally operated drug store. Upon arrival at the store the police found the defendant inside the store in the men's restroom. There was evidence of forced entry through a rear door. Defendant was arrested without incident and booked into the county jail. He did not have any firearm or other deadly weapon on him at the time of his arrest, nor did he have any burglary tools. He did not have in his possession any items from the store at the time of his arrest. A tire iron was located outside of the rear door and was later determined to have the defendant's fingerprints on one end. The wood particles on the end of the tire iron matched the wood of the door frame through which entry of the building was made.

Summary of Court Proceedings:

Defendant pled not guilty, was assigned a public defender, went to trial before a jury, and was found guilty of commercial burglary.

Defendant's Version of the Offense:

Defendant has consistently stated that he did not burglarize the store. He claims that he was in the area of the store when he started feeling sick. He noticed that the rear door of the store was open and he went in to use the restroom. He did not testify on his own behalf at the trial, but in his statement made for purposes of this report he claims he does not know why the tire iron from his vehicle would have been in the alley by the rear entrance of the store other than that it must have been stolen from his vehicle.

Defendant's Background

Juvenile Record:	None located; defendant states he was never arrested by the police when he was a juvenile but that he was on juvenile probation for truancy, but no record was found		
Adult Record:	07/05/2002	Possession of Marijuana Wellsville, Ohio	18 months' unsupervised probation; successful discharge
	04/22/2005	Possession of Cocaine Wellsville, Ohio	Drug Court and three years' probation; successful discharge

Financial Condition:

Savings:	None
Assets:	None
Liabilities:	$375 per month rent for apartment lease shared with male friend

$243 per month car payment; $7652 balance
$97 per month car insurance
Approximately $150 per month shared utility costs

Family:

The defendant is the only child of James and Marie Doe. Parents divorced when defendant was two years old. Father remarried six months after divorce and has three children with second wife. James Doe relocated to California soon after the divorce and relinquished all visitation privileges, as stated in the divorce decree. Defendant's father regularly paid $300 per month child support until defendant reached the age of 21. Defendant states that he has never seen his biological father since the divorce. Defendant states that he maintained a close and amiable relationship with his mother throughout his childhood and to present day. He describes her as hardworking and caring but frequently absent from the home due to work responsibilities. The defendant states he has lived with a variety of friends since he turned 21 years of age, but he maintains regular contact with his mother through home visits and phone calls. He states that she has visited with him at the jail twice weekly since his incarceration.

Marital Status:

Never married

Co-dependents:

None

Medical:

Defendant states that he has not in the past and does not presently experience any physical or mental health difficulties, nor is he on any prescribed medication.

Military:

Never in the military

Addictions:

Defendant claims no addictions. He states that the prior drug related arrests were a result of his occasional recreational use of marijuana and cocaine.

Education:

> Defendant has a high school diploma. He states he never went to college and has no interest in continuing his education. He further stated that he graduated from high school a year later than expected due to shortage of credit hours earned, which resulted in the need to retake several previously failed classes. He achieved a 2.1 GPA from high school.

Employment:

> Defendant started working part-time temporary jobs in construction at the age of 16. He has continued to work temporary construction jobs throughout his adult life although some of the work has been full time. He explained that when he does not have a steady construction job he works part-time temporary home improvement jobs, mainly in painting and dry wall for a variety of local businesses owned mainly by friends and families of friends.

Summary

John Doe is a 28-year-old white male who was born in Wellsville, Ohio, where he has remained throughout his life. He currently resides with a male friend. He has never been married and does not have any children. He has a high school diploma and no earned college credit or trade school education. He has worked at a variety of construction jobs, mainly part-time and temporary employment. He has also worked doing home repair as part-time and temporary jobs when he can locate the work. He has two prior felony arrests as an adult, both drug related. He successfully completed the required probation terms for both of these sentences and also was successfully discharged from the county drug court program. No juvenile record was located.

Recommendation to the Court

It is hereby recommended to the Court that the defendant be sentenced to _____

Note: This is where the probation officer responsible for writing the report indicates what he/she recommends the sentence within the restrictions of the statutes and taking into consideration the circumstances of the case and the defendant's background. The recommendation commonly includes suggested interventions, such as counseling, education, vocational training, community service, restitution, etc. Recommending length of time under correctional supervision is appropriate, but neither specific institutional placement (security level), nor specific length of parole supervision is to be included in the recommendation, as these are functions of the corrections department and not the judicial system.

Assignment 6.1

1. What would you recommend for sentence to the Court? Be sure to word it in language appropriate to a formal sentencing proceeding and within the statutes, based on the information presented in the case.

2. Do you think that the defendant should receive credit for the 102 days he has been in jail, time served, toward a reduction of whatever sentence he is given? Why or why not?

3. The present conviction is John Doe's third felony. If this case occurred in a state with a three strikes law, do you think that the appropriate sentence should be life in prison? Why or why not? Explain the reasons for your position, including information from the case.

4. In what type of sentencing might a judge require a presentencing report? What elements of the sentencing type would allow for including a presentencing report? In what type of sentencing would a presentencing report not be an option? What elements of the sentencing type would not allow for including a presentencing report?

5. What additional information should be included in a presentencing report that would be beneficial to the sentencing decision? Explain your answer.

6. Do you think that judges who require presentencing reports should ask for a recommendation? Why or why not?

Probation Violation Report

Convicted offenders sentenced to serve time on probation are required to abide by two basic categories of conditions: (1) they must not commit any new felony or misdemeanor offense, and (2) they must abide by technical conditions. The technical conditions of a probation order commonly include the following:

1.   Must notify the probation officer within 48 hours of a change of residence
2.   Must gain and maintain steady employment within 30 days of being placed on probation
3.   Must not own or possess any firearm or other deadly weapon
4.   Must notify the probation officer of a change in employment status within 48 hours of that change
5.   Must not leave the county of residence without obtaining a travel permit from the probation department
6.   Must not associate with other known felons
7.   Must not frequent known liquor establishments
8.   Must not use, have in possession, deal, or traffic in any illegal controlled substance
9.   Must follow all additional requirements of probation as dictated by the probation department, including attending and/or completing counseling programs, enrolling in educational and/or vocational programs, and following restrictions in residential and work-related placements

Although likely to be worded slightly differently, depending on the county and the state where the probation office operates, the conditions of probation tend to be similar to those stated above.

The main purpose of the condition prohibiting the client from any new offense is to provide for any necessary and immediate incarceration of the probation client pending the resolution of the new charges, the focus being on public safety. The general technical conditions of probation (1–9) are to assist in the surveillance of the client as well as to promote the safety of the probation officers and the public. The purpose of specific conditions, as dictated in the language used in "9" are intended to provide intervention services to decrease the likelihood of recidivism. The conditions placed on the client would be specific to the individual case.

The actual procedure followed for revocation of probation depends on the jurisdiction of the probation department and the regulations specific to that judicial system. In general, if a probation client commits subsequent felony or misdemeanor crime, the court must be notified immediately by means of the probation violation report. Decisions about violations of technical conditions are more subjective and often rely on the informal rules of the individual probation office and sometimes of the individual officers. For example, one particular probation office may follow an informal policy that allows clients two urine screens that test positive for illegal substances before submitting a violation report to the court. Another probation office may follow a policy that a probation violation report must be submitted to the court on any urine screen that tests positive for an illegal substance. Officers within a probation office may even differ in the discretion used for making decisions about probation violations. For example, one officer may write a violation report notifying the court of a client's violation of the condition to notify the officer within 48 hours of a change of residence. Another officer, in the same probation office, may decide not to write a violation report of a client with the same condition violation. Officers new to the job are well-advised to gather preliminary information about the norms of the specific probation office regarding violation reports of technical conditions. These norms are commonly dictated by the preferences of the judges who decide on the violation reports and, sometimes, those who work in the prosecutor's office.

Like the presentencing report, recommendations may be included as part of the violation report, but their inclusion is at the discretion of the local judiciary. Some judges want the recommendation to be included, other judges prefer to hear the probation officer's recommendation at the time of the sentencing hearing, while other judges prefer no recommendation be made by the probation officer or department. It is important to know that the outcome of the probation violation report is a judiciary function. Depending on the type of sentencing used in the jurisdiction of the probation, as well as the statutes regulating probation violations, the judge may choose among the following general options for a violation: (1) revoke the original sentence of probation and sentence the person to prison for the time allowed in the statute (the person may or may not receive credit for time already served on probation), (2) place the person back on probation with additional conditions required, (3) order the person to a period of jail time, followed by continuation of probation, (4) order the person to an extended jail period with no condition of probation upon release, (5) order the person returned to probation with the original conditions pending the conclusion of the new charge, or (6) return the person to probation with no additional conditions and no required incarceration in jail or prison.

Example Probation Violation Report

(This exercise uses the information of John Doe, presented in the example presentencing report).

Date:	September 12, 2010
Name of Probationer:	John Doe
Original Offense:	Commercial Burglary — Felony C
Original Sentence:	Three years' incarceration to be served in a state penitentiary, all suspended. Offender placed on supervised probation for a period of three years; no credit for time served in jail prior to sentencing
Date placed on probation:	February 7, 2010
Amount of time served on probation:	217 days (approximately 7 months)
Sentencing Judge:	Honorable Joseph Smith
Probation Officer:	Curt Karl

Facts of the Violation

The Wellsville Police Department notified the probation department on September 10, 2010, that John Doe had been arrested for possession of marijuana on said date. Mr. Doe had been stopped by the police for speeding on County Road 16 at 2:47 p.m. on September 10, 2010. The officer smelled marijuana and asked Mr. Doe to step out of the vehicle. When he stepped out of the vehicle, a baggie of what appeared to be marijuana dropped out of the vehicle. Mr. Doe was arrested and taken to the county jail and was booked on the charge of possession of marijuana.

Compliance with Probation Conditions

Mr. Doe has been on probation for approximately 7 months. He has reported in once every two weeks as required by his probation officer. A urine sample taken on 2/8/10, when he signed the probation conditions, tested negative for any illegal substances. A urine sample taken on 2/22/10 tested positive for cannabis. Subsequent urine screens on 3/26/10, 4/16/10, 5/3/10, 6/10/10, 7/14/10, and 8/21/10 all tested negative. Mr. Doe has attended group substance abuse counseling sessions once a week, as ordered in the specific probation conditions. He recently began taking classes at the local junior college in the heating, venting, and air conditioning trade program. He has paid all of his required monthly probation fees.

Recommendation to the Court

It is hereby recommended to the Court that the probationer, John Doe, be

_____

Assignment 6.2

1. What would you recommend to the Court? Explain your reasoning, being sure to include information from the original presentencing report, as well as information contained in the violation report.

2. If the decision of the court is to continue Mr. Doe on probation, with or without some jail time required, what do you think are his chances of successfully completing his probationary term? Explain your answer.

3. If the decision of the court is to sentence Mr. Doe for an extended period of jail time with no follow-up probation, what do you think his chances are of not recidivating with any new arrest for a period of three years after release from jail? Explain your answer.

4. If the court decides to sentence Mr. Doe to prison for the three years he was originally sentenced to probation, what do you think his chances are of not recidivating with any new arrest for the period of three years after release? Explain your answer.

5. Do you think that the original sentence that Mr. Doe received was the correct choice in sentencing? Explain your answer.

6. If you were to recommend that Mr. Doe be returned to probation with added specific conditions, what should those conditions be? Explain your rationale.

7. If Mr. Doe is sentenced to prison for violating the probation conditions, do you think that he should receive credit for time served on probation? In other words, if he is sentenced to three years in prison, should the sentence automatically be reduced by the 217 days he has been on probation? Explain your answer.

8. Do you think that judges should require a recommendation from the probation officer supervising the case as part of the probation violation report? Why or why not?

9. Would your answer to question #1 above be different if the same circumstances for the offense occurred but it was a gram or less of cocaine wrapped in plastic that dropped out of the vehicle when Mr. Doe was ordered from the car? Why or why not?

10. Do you think that the judge should wait to make a decision on the probation violation until after the current charge of possession of marijuana is processed through the court? Why or why not? Explain your answer.

Alternative Probation Violation Report

(This exercise uses the information of John Doe, presented in the example presentencing report).

Date:	September 12, 2010
Name of Probationer:	John Doe
Original Offense:	Commercial Burglary—Felony C
Original Sentence:	Three years' incarceration, to be served in a state penitentiary, all suspended. Offender placed on supervised probation for a period of three years; no credit for time served in jail prior to sentencing
Date placed on probation:	February 7, 2010

Amount of time   217 days (approximately 7 months)
served on probation:

Basis for Issuance of Violation Report

Urine screens testing positive for cannabis: 2/8/10, 4/12/10, and 6/02/10
Failure to attend six regularly scheduled group counseling sessions
Travel out of the county without a travel permit
Failure to notify probation officer within 48 hours of residential relocation

Summary of Case Notes

Although Mr. Doe has regularly reported in as required by his probation officer and is up to date on his required probation fees, he has violated a number of other technical and specific conditions, as noted above. However, Mr. Doe has maintained gainful employment and presents as an individual who is not a threat to public safety. There are no reports of any new misdemeanor or felony arrests, and an NCIC check verified this information. Nor is there any evidence that Mr. Doe is frequenting known liquor establishments, associating with other known felons, or has in his possession a firearm or other deadly weapon.

Recommendation to the Court

It is hereby recommended to the Court that the probationer, John Doe, be

---

Assignment 6.3

1. What would you recommend to the Court? Explain your reasoning, being sure to include information from the original presentencing report, as well as information contained in this alternative violation report.

2. If the decision of the court is to continue Mr. Doe on probation, with or without some jail time required, what do you think are his chances of successfully completing his probationary term? Explain your answer.

3. If the decision of the court is to sentence Mr. Doe for an extended period of jail time with no follow-up probation, what do you think are his chances of not recidivating with any new arrest for three years after release from jail? Explain your answer.

4. If the decision of the court is to sentence Mr. Doe to prison for the three years he was originally sentenced to probation, what do you think are his chances of not recidivating with any new arrest for three years after release? Explain your answer.

5. If you were to recommend that Mr. Doe be placed back on probation with added specific conditions, what should those conditions be? Explain your rationale.

6. If Mr. Doe is sentenced to prison for violating the probation conditions, do you think that he should receive credit for time served on probation? In other words if he is sentenced to three years in prison, should the sentence automatically be reduced by the 217 days he has been on probation? Explain your answer.

7. Do you think the court should be notified of the violations of probation conditions as noted above in this alternative report? Why or why not? Explain.

8. Do you think that the urine screens testing positive for cannabis hold more weight in regards to violating conditions than the other technical violations committed? Explain your answer.

9. Should the judge have the option of lifting the original sentence of probation and sentencing offenders who commit technical violations to prison? Why or why not? Explain your answer.

10. Should a probation violation report be submitted to the court, based on the information of this case? Why or why not?

11. Should probation departments have a standard policy on when to submit a violation report to the court for violations of technical conditions? In other words, should the decision be left to the probation officer, or should a consistent policy be used in attempts to remove subjective decisions? Explain your answer. Do you think a standard policy would remove subjective decisions? Explain your answer.

12. Do you think that John Doe is a risk to public safety? Explain your answer, using information from the alternative probation violation report and information in the PSR.

Parole Violation Reports

As you have probably learned already, parole is supervision of an offender in the community after s/he has served time in a correctional facility (prison). As with probation, the main purpose of parole supervision is public safety. There is usually very little difference in the conditions for parole or probation. However, parole officers usually have a caseload of offenders who were convicted of more serious offenses than officers supervising probation caseloads. The fact that the client has been incarcerated in a correctional facility often makes the supervision of the parole client somewhat different from supervision of the probation client because the parole client must be reintegrated into community living. Also the stigma attached to having served time in prison is commonly difficult to overcome for parolees, even though both probationers and parolees are, in most cases, convicted felons. During incarceration the offender may have lost employment and/or family placement. Depending on the length of time of incarceration, the client may have difficulties adjusting to living in the free society. All of these factors increase the difficulties the client may have in complying with the legal and technical conditions of parole.

A major distinction between the probation revocation process and the parole revocation process is that probation violation reports are addressed through the judicial branch whereas parole violation reports are addressed through the executive branch of government, that being the state corrections department. Whereas a probation violation report is filed with the court of original jurisdiction, the parole violation report is filed with the state corrections department parole division. Commonly, the first step after a parole violation report is submitted is to have a hearing by a regional supervisor after which, if the finding is that a violation occurred, the offender is transported to the corrections department for the final decision to be made by the parole board. Yet another difference is that parole violators, by nature of the seriousness of the original offense for which they were incarcerated and the strong likelihood that his or her parole will be revoked resulting in return to prison, are usually considered a higher risk of flight and risk to public safety. Therefore, a parole violator is likely to be arrested for parole violation at the time the violation is noted and held in custody in the county jail throughout the initial hearing process. Of course, whether this occurs depends on the specifics of the individual case and the jurisdiction overseeing the parole supervision.

In summary, the differences between a probation violation report and a parole violation report are: (1) probation violations are addressed through the judiciary, whereas parole violations are addressed through the state corrections department, (2) parolees must be reintegrated into the free society, (3) the stigma attached to a parolee of being labeled an "ex-con" can, and often does, have consequences on employment opportunities, (4) parolees have frequently been convicted of more serious offenses than probationers, and (5) the likelihood of a parole violator being sent to prison is higher than the likelihood of a probation violator, and thus the risk for flight and risk to public safety is likely to be higher, as well.

Example Parole Violation Report

(This exercise uses the information of John Doe presented in the example presentencing report. The dates reflect future projection based on a sentence to prison.)

Date:	May 7, 2012
Name of Probationer:	John Doe
Original Offense:	Commercial Burglary — Felony C
Original Sentence:	Three years' incarceration to be served in a state penitentiary; no credit for time served in jail prior to sentencing
Sentencing Date:	February 20, 2010
Date placed on parole:	November 15, 2011
Amount of time served on parole:	170 days (approximately 5½ months)

John Doe served a little over 1½ years of a 3-year prison sentence. He was housed in a minimum security prison. The report from the prison that came with the parole packet indicates that he did not have any disciplinary reports while in prison. He was released after serving half his original prison sentence due to the state's good time policy of a day earned off the sentence for every day served without disciplinary actions. While in prison, Mr. Doe participated with several work crews, originally with roadside cleanup and later with prison maintenance. He did not participate in any educational or vocational training programs, but he did regularly attend a substance abuse group counseling program that was facilitated by volunteers from the community.

Basis for Issuance of Violation Report

Arrest for Possession of Marijuana

Summary of Case Notes

Mr. Doe was arrested for possession of marijuana on May 3, 2012. The police responded to complaints of a loud party by neighbors in a residential area. Upon arrival, the police discovered approximately 25 individuals in the backyard of one of the residences. They were playing various yard games, such as volleyball and catch football. Music blared loudly from the stereo speakers on the patio. There appeared to be minors consuming alcoholic beverages. When the police asked for identifications from every person at the location, as Mr. Doe removed his wallet from his back pocket, a small baggie of what appeared to contain cannabis fell to the ground. Mr. Doe was arrested, and the parole office was notified after it was discovered, through reading the material contained in his wallet, that Mr. Doe was currently on parole. The amount of cannabis in the baggie was enough for approximately three joints. He was charged with a misdemeanor punishable by 6 months and/or a $1,000 fine. Several minors were taken into custody at the same time that Mr. Doe was arrested, their parents were notified, and reports were submitted to the juvenile probation department for minors in possession of alcohol. Mr. Doe voluntarily took a breathalyzer test, which recorded a blood alcohol content of .06.

Mr. Doe has reported to the parole office as required. He is current on all of his fees, including those charged for urine screens. Six urine screens have tested negative for illegal substances. Mr. Doe has been residing with his mother since his release from prison. He has not located any employment and has followed the requirement of the parole officer that he register with the government operated employment development program. He has provided required proof of his search for employment. Because of the faltering economy, the construction and home repair employment opportunities decreased dramatically while Mr. Doe was in prison. Mr. Doe has regularly attended group substance abuse counseling at the county-operated free clinic.

Mr. Doe is currently in jail on an order from the parole office until conclusion of the current violation report.

Recommendation

It is hereby recommended that the parolee, John Doe, be _____

Assignment 6.4

1. What would you recommend at the regional parole hearing? Be specific on your recommendation.

2. John Doe is now 30 years old. He is having difficulties finding employment and is living at home with his mother. If the decision is to keep Mr. Doe on parole, what additional conditions are needed to improve the chances that he will not recidivate?

3. Do you think that Mr. Doe is a risk to public safety? Why or why not? Explain your answer.

4. Do you think that Mr. Doe's revocation hearing should take place prior to the resolution of the current possession of marijuana charge? Why or why not? Explain your answer.

5. In the state where Mr. Doe resides, the average cost of incarceration is approximately $28,000 a year. Do you think that revoking his parole, based on his history and current charge, is worth the cost of incarceration for the remainder of his original sentence (approximately 18 months)? Justify your response in terms of monetary costs and deterrent value, both general and specific.

6. Do you think that convicted felons on parole should have parole revoked for a new misdemeanor offense? Why or why not?

Case Notes

Probation and parole officers are required to keep a log of all contacts made in reference to a case, including contact with the client through office appointments, home visits, employment checks, verification of attendance at counseling sessions and court-ordered educational or vocational training, and phone calls from the client, to name but a few examples. Notes should be kept of any information that is provided to the officer about the client, such as through phone calls from family members, police department inquiries pertaining to the client, employers, counselors, or calls from significant others or friends reporting information about the client. It is critically important that case notes be recorded as soon as possible after the contact is made to ensure accuracy and to keep the record up to date. Because probation and parole officers have many, many cases to supervise at one time, they should not rely on memory and plan on catching up on case notes at a later time, such as once a week.

The officers must rely on the case notes to assemble a report, if needed, such as a violation report. They also need to rely on their notes if they are called into court to testify in a particular case or are questioned by another agency regarding the involvement of a client in various activities. It is important to know that if the officer takes a hard copy of case notes to a formal hearing or court proceeding, the case notes may be admitted as evidence. Knowing this possibility, the officer must remember to be accurate, clear, and comprehensive but yet concise in recording the notes. It is not appropriate to record judgment or opinions about a client or to speculate without supporting information. It is important to accurately record the facts of dates and times that contact was made with or about a client, including the length of time of that contact. The following abbreviated example is included to assist the reader in better understanding how important accuracy is.

Scott is a probation officer who supervises Belinda, who was placed on probation for child endangerment for leaving her 18-month-old son in her vehicle when she went into a bar to join friends for drinks on a Saturday afternoon. Scott has a very heavy caseload and a habit of catching up on notes over the weekend. He records that he saw Belinda the previous Tuesday, May 3 at 3:00 p.m. for her monthly required office visit and that he chatted with her for 10 minutes. A few days after making these case notes, Scott is contacted by a police officer, who asks him if he has any record of where Belinda was on Tuesday, May 3 at approximately 3:00 p.m. Scott looks over his notes and advises the police officer that Belinda was meeting with him at the probation office. The police are asking about Scott's knowledge of Belinda's whereabouts on that particular day and at that time because they received a report from someone who saw a young child alone in a vehicle in the parking lot outside a bar on that day and at that approximate time. This information came to the attention of the police days after the alleged occurrence when they were following up on a hit-and-run of a vehicle that occurred in the parking lot on the same day and at the same time and were questioning some individuals who frequent that particular bar on a regular basis. One of the officers involved in the investigation recognized the description of the car with the child as matching the description of the car in a previous arrest for child endangerment. After this explanation as to why the police are asking about Belinda's whereabouts, Scott gives more thought to whether or not he accurately recorded the date and time of Belinda's visit to his office. He is concerned that he may have confused the date or time of the visit.

This example illustrates the importance of the accuracy of case notes. An officer cannot know what future events may occur that the notes recorded about contacts with or about clients will be the basis for additional criminal investigation.

The following example of case notes is based on the case of John Doe, as summarized in the alternative probation violation report provided in a previous section of this chapter.

Example Case Notes — John Doe

Name of Probationer: John Doe

Original Offense: Commercial Burglary — Felony C

Original Sentence: Three years' incarceration, to be served in a state penitentiary, all suspended. Offender placed on supervised probation for a period of three years; no credit for time served in jail prior to sentencing

Date placed on probation: February 7, 2010

Date	Notes
February 8, 2010 2:14 p.m.	Client reported in for first time. Officer read the probation conditions to the client asking the client after each condition if he had any questions. The client did not have any questions and signed the probation conditions, indicating he understood the conditions and agreed to abide with all conditions. Officer went through the probation risk and needs assessment with the client. Based on the total points, the client will be under maximum supervision, required to report to the probation office once every other week and one additional contact with the client (phone call or home visit) weekly, for the first three months of his probation after which he will be re-evaluated to determine whether he should stay on maximum supervision or have the supervision level changed. Client provided a urine screen.
February 12, 2010	Lab results indicated urine screen of client taken on 2/8/10 tested positive for cannabis. Results from the lab have been filed in client's hard-copy file.
February 13, 2010 8:30 a.m.	Phone message left at client's home number on the answering machine, requesting that client contact the probation department as soon as possible.
February 14, 2010 10:20 a.m.	Phone message left at client's home number on the answering machine, requesting that client contact the probation department as soon as possible.
February 15, 2010 4:10 p.m.	Phone message left at client's home number on the answering machine, requesting that client contact the probation department as soon as possible.
February 22, 2010 3:10 p.m.	Client reported in to the office at two-week interval as required. When asked if he received the three phone messages left at his home address, he told the officer that he just heard the messages the night before, after he returned home from visiting a friend in Michigan. Officer reminded the client that he was required to receive a travel permit if

leaving the county. Client said he "forgot about that condition." He apologized and said it would not happen again. Client was given instructions for attending a substance abuse counseling group at a local free clinic once a week for 12 weeks. The clinic offers numerous time options four days a week, including Saturdays.

February 26, 2010
7:20 p.m.

Officer went to client's listed residence at 7:20 p.m. Client was at home watching television. He said that he had picked up a temporary construction job through the business of a friend and that he was working from 7:00 a.m. to about 6:00 p.m. daily.

March 5, 2010
4:50 p.m.

Client reported to the probation office as required. He provided a urine specimen. He said that the temporary construction job had finished but that he has a lead on another job involving dry wall work in an office building.

March 9, 2010

Lab results indicated urine screen of client taken on 3/5/10 tested negative for alcohol or any illegal substances. Results from the lab have been filed in client's hard copy file.

March 12, 2010
9:10 p.m.

Officer contacted counseling clinic to determine if client registered for the group counseling sessions and attended at least one session. He was told that the client had attended one session since February 22. He did not attend a session the weeks of March 1 and March 8.

March 18, 2010
3:30 p.m.

Client reported to the probation office as required. Officer asked him about his attendance at the substance abuse groups. Client told the officer he knows he missed two weeks but that he had picked up the dry wall work and was busy. Officer reminded client that the clinic is open on Saturdays. Client says he works Saturdays. Officer told client that he is now required to bring in verification from a work supervisor of the hours and days he works. Client said "No problem."

March 23, 2010
9:30 p.m.

Officer went to client's listed residence at 9:30 p.m. Client did not answer door, and his vehicle was not visible at the residence.

March 25, 2010
10:45 p.m.

Officer went to client's listed residence at 10:45 p.m. Client did not answer door, and his vehicle was not visible at the residence.

March 26, 2010
8:10 a.m.

Officer attempted to make contact with the client by phone call to his home number. The phone has been disconnected. Officer left a message at the client's listed cell phone number, requesting that he contact the probation department.

March 30, 2010
10:10 a.m.

Client phoned officer. Officer asked him about the disconnected home phone line. Client told officer that he had to move out because he could not pay the next month's rent. He said that he was staying with a friend and gave the officer the new address. He explained that there was no home phone number to contact and that this was likely to be a temporary living arrangement. Officer told client he was required to report to the office the next day.

March 31, 2010
4:25 p.m.

Client called officer to ask permission to report in the coming week. He said he had a new job and would bring in verification of employment when he reported in. Officer reminded him about his requirement to attend group counseling sessions. Client apologized for not attending but explained that he had been busy trying to locate work and moving from his apartment to live with a friend. He said he would report in to the office on April 5, even if he had to miss work to come in. Officer gave him permission to come in on April 5 but told him he needed to attend the group session on Saturday, April 3.

April 5, 2010
9:30 a.m./7:00 p.m.

Officer made contact with the counseling clinic and verified that client did attend a session on April 3. Client called to explain that he would report in after work at approximately 7:00 p.m. Officer agreed to meet him at the office at 7:00. Client reported in and brought with him verification of employment from the construction supervisor in the form of a letter, on letterhead, from the supervisor about the hours worked the past week. Officer reminded client that he was to report residential changes within 48 hours. Client stated it had "slipped his mind" because he was so busy trying to find a place to live and to pack. He apologized. Officer reminded client that he was required to attend counseling sessions once a week. Client said that he would "try harder."

April 12, 2010
8:10 p.m.

Officer went to the client's listed place of residence at 8:10 p.m. Client was at the residence of a friend. Officer requested a urine specimen and the client provided one.

April 15, 2010

Lab results of the urine specimen indicated a positive test for cannabis. The hard copy of the lab result was placed in the client's file.

April 19, 2010
11:45 a.m.

Client called officer to say that he had to work late and would not be able to come in to the office to report. He gave the officer the supervisor's contact number to verify this information, which the officer did. Officer left a message on the client's cell phone number that he must arrange his work hours to report in after work on April 21. Client said he would do that.

April 21, 2010
7:35 p.m.

Client reported in after work at 7:35 p.m. Officer told the client that the urine specimen on April 12 tested positive for cannabis. Client said that he "slipped up." He was at the friend's apartment and they were watching a movie and had some other guys over and he smoked a "little." Officer summarized for the client that he now had two urine tests that were positive for cannabis, that he had traveled out of the county without permission, and that he had moved without notifying the probation office within 48 hours — all of these in direct violation of his probation conditions. Client told the officer he will "try harder." He reminded the officer that he has been working, has reported in as told, has paid his probation fees, and has been attending counseling sessions once a week since April 3. He said that he is trying to save enough money to move into his own apartment. Officer reminded him he has to notify the probation office within 48 hours of a change of address.

Officer told client that one more violation of conditions and he will send a violation report to the Judge.

April 26, 2010
8:30 a.m.

Officer verified with the counseling clinic that client has been attending group counseling sessions once a week since April 3.

May 5, 2010
5:35 p.m.

Client reported in as required. The construction job that he has been working will be finished the end of this week. Client is seeking other work. He is still living in same location. He provided a urine specimen.

May 10, 2010

Lab results indicated that the urine specimen tested negative for any controlled substances. The hard copy of the lab result was placed in the client's file.

May 12, 2010
9:35 p.m.

Officer went to client's listed place of residence at 9:35 p.m. No one answered the door and the client's vehicle was not visible.

May 17, 2010
4:20 p.m.

Client reported to the probation office. He told officer that he has been so busy looking for work that he totally forgot to attend the last two weeks of counseling. He said he would get a session in during the week. He stated that he is at the same residence. He has not been able to locate work.

May 25, 2010
9:50 a.m.

Officer contacted the counseling clinic and was told that the client did attend a session during the week of May 17.

May 28, 2010
8:35 a.m.

Client came to the office to ask permission to travel to Michigan to visit with family over the holiday weekend. He provided the address where he would be staying, as well as two phone contact numbers and names of relatives where he will be staying. He was provided a travel permit to return on June 1. He was told to report to the office on June 2.

June 2, 2010
3:20 p.m.

Client reported as required. He has not been able to find work. He told officer that he may request to relocate to live with relatives in Michigan because his uncle told him he could find him work on a farm in the area. He said he wanted to relocate to find work but also that he wants to live with family rather than with the person he has been staying with. He was told that he would have to bring verification of opportunity for steady gainful employment before the officer would make the request for an interstate transfer of probation supervision and that place of residence would have to be verified through the Michigan probation office in the county where he is intending to live. Officer obtained a urine specimen.

June 7, 2010 — Lab results indicated that the urine specimen tested positive for cannabis. Officer compiled a probation violation report and sent it to the prosecutor's office and the district court judge.

Assignment 6.5

1. Do the case notes provide the evidence for the violations as listed in the alternative violation report? Provide the case note dates and information that support the violation report.

2. Do you think that Mr. Doe was given too many chances by his probation officer? Explain the reasoning for your position.

3. If you were Mr. Doe's officer, what would you have done differently in the management of his case? Be sure to describe fully the type of restrictions or requirements you would have made, as well as decisions on noted violations. Explain your reasoning.

4. Do you think that the probation officer's supervision of Mr. Doe was appropriate to the case? Explain your answer.

Parole Plan

It is important to know that not all states have parole as an option under their state corrections policies and statutes. For those states that continue to use parole (supervised community placement after release from a correctional facility), the information contained in a parole plan pertains to the offender's projected place of residence and employment after release. Case managers at the facilities obtain this information from the inmate and complete a request that the information be verified. This request is commonly forwarded to the parole office that is closest to the area where the inmate plans to parole. How this verification of information is completed depends on the policies of the particular state. A common practice is for the assigned parole officer to visit the indicated address and talk with the residents to ensure that they are aware that the inmate has indicated that s/he is intending to live at that location. Verifying employment as indicated by the inmate is commonly conducted through a phone call or by contacting the indicated employer in person.

A great deal of information can be gained through these on-site visits by the parole officer. For example, the officer may learn that the address for the residence does not exist or the address indicated is, in fact, the location of a supermarket or car dealership. In making contact with current residents at the indicated address, the officer may learn that they do not know the inmate or, if known, they never agreed to have the inmate live with them and would object to such a placement. These situations are not the norm, but do occur from time to time. Ideally, the officer will learn that the residents are aware that the inmate is soon to be paroled, that s/he is welcome, and that the indicated employer verifies that a job is waiting for the inmate upon release. In the majority of parole plans, a residence is secured but employment is not. If the inmate does not have a verified place to live after release, the parole plan may be rejected and sent back to the department of corrections for notification to the inmate's case manager. The process is likely to start all over again with a new address of potential residence upon release. Occasionally, an inmate remains incarcerated for what would have been the parole period and is released at the expiration date, unsupervised in the community.

Without doubt, verifying information contained in the parole plan is not only in the best interest of public safety but also assists the inmate in establishing stability in plans for release. One can imagine how devastating it would be for an inmate to be paroled to a family that no longer agrees to have any contact with him or her. At that point, s/he would be homeless with few resources and very likely limited coping skills to deal with such a situation.

The following example parole plan is provided to assist the reader in better understanding what may occur during the verification process and how important following through in checking the information provided is.

Example Parole Plan

Bryant is currently incarcerated in a maximum security correctional facility on a conviction for aggravated robbery of a convenience store with a handgun. He was sentenced to 22 years, of which he has served 15 years and 3 months, all at the same facility. The time to be served was reduced from 22 years, due to the good time policies in the state. In fact, he received day-for-day good time credit but, due to a total of six disciplinary reports, for engaging in assaultive behavior of other inmates, his good time credit has been reduced by approximately four years. He has a projected release date in six months. He is currently participating in the prerelease program and may be released sooner, based on the overcrowding in the facility. As a result, the case manager of the facility who worked with Bryant over the past two years has compiled a parole plan.

Bryant has indicated that he will parole to his uncle's home, a residence in the county of his conviction. Also residing in the home are his uncle's girlfriend and her three children, ages 17 (son), 15 (son), and 12 (daughter). Bryant states that he has an employment placement upon release at a construction company, assisting with installing heating, venting, and air conditioning units in businesses. The job, part of the tax credit program that employers receive for hiring ex-offenders, was arranged through contact between the construction company and the transition officer employed by the state department of corrections.

Assignment 6.6

1. If you were the parole officer assigned to verifying projected residence information for the parole plan, would you use telephone contact or a personal visit to the residence? Explain your answer, providing the reasons for your choice.

2. If you were the parole officer assigned to verifying projected employment placement information for the parole plan, would you use telephone contact or a personal visit to the employer? Explain your answer providing the reasons for your choice.

3. What questions would you ask Bryant's uncle and, possibly, the other residents of the home about the projected residential placement? Make a list of your questions and state briefly why they are important questions to ask.

4. What questions would you ask the projected employer? Make a list of the questions and state briefly why they are important questions to ask.

5. If the projected residential placement is verified but the projected employment is not, would you approve the parole plan or reject it? Explain your answer, providing your rationale.

6. What information about the projected residential placement would lead you to reject the parole plan, even if Bryant's uncle clearly states that Bryant is welcome to live with him? Explain your answer.

Community Corrections Programs

An outcome of the focus on the challenges of reintegrating an offender back into the community and a need to limit the increasingly overcrowded conditions in the nation's correctional facilities of the 1970s and 1980s led to a number of states developing community corrections programs. Many of the legislative acts that created these programs pertained mainly to the composition and role of a community corrections advisory board in reference to overseeing community corrections creation and operation. However, some of the acts also allowed for an opportunity of community representatives to have a "voice" in whether or not an offender was given a sentence that allowed him or her to stay in the community. In these acts the language that specifies the protocol for referrals and the screening process also stipulate that if the community corrections advisory board refuses to accept a referred offender for community placement, the sentencing judge has no option but to order the offender incarcerated in jail or prison. The requirements for the composition of the board and the number of members vary by jurisdiction. Commonly, the board consists of representatives from law enforcement, the legal field, counseling services, area businesses, the religious community, employment services, and educational providers. Often a representative from the county probation office or a representative from an agency created to oversee the community corrections in the county receives the referrals, tracks all required paperwork, and organizes and facilitates the meeting when the case is discussed. Although the names for such programs may have changed over the years, the original intent and design remains the same.

In most cases, the defense attorney makes the request for a referral to the community corrections board. The packet provided to the board members, usually at least a week in advance of a scheduled meeting, commonly includes the presentencing report, police reports, the psychological evaluation, if appropriate, and relevant assessments pertaining to education and employment. The agency in charge of overseeing the involvement of the community corrections advisory board makes contact with each member to arrange a time to meet, with an effort to get 100% attendance at the meeting.

As illustrated in the example below, the referral is frequently a summary of key points. The information in the summary is supplemented with all the additional information included in the packet. It is the process of involving representatives from the community in making a decision that influences the offender's sentence that distinguishes these cases from others handled by the court.

Example Community Corrections Program Referral

Plea/Conviction:	December 29, 2009
Referral Date:	January 5, 2010
Party Making Referral:	Bill White, Defense Attorney
Sentencing Hearing:	January 26, 2010
Name of Offender:	James Clark
Age:	27
Gender:	Male
Race:	African American

Offense: Voluntary Manslaughter: punishable by 10 years in a state penitentiary followed by two years supervised parole

Summary of Offense: On May 16, 2009 Mr. Clark was at the Buzz In Tavern, located at 101 S. 66th Street, Southtown. An argument ensued between Mr. Clark and Mr. Jones, a patron, over the music choice playing on the jukebox. This verbal argument became increasingly heated with profanity used and threats of bodily injury being made by both parties. The two men started fist fighting and kicking each other. One of the contact punches that Mr. Jones made on Mr. Clark resulted in Mr. Clark's being knocked to the ground, after which Mr. Jones straddled Mr. Clark. At this point, Mr. Clark pulled a 22-caliber revolver from his waistband and shot Mr. Jones in the face with three separate shots. Twelve customers, as well as one of the bartenders, witnessed the shooting. A second bartender and manager of the Tavern had been on the phone calling 911 after the fight broke out and did not witness the shooting. Although emergency medical technicians arrived at the scene at approximately the same time as the police units, Mr. Jones was dead by the time they arrived. Mr. Clark voluntarily took a breathalyzer test at the time of booking that recorded a .06 blood alcohol content. A urine screen obtained also at booking tested negative for any illegal substances.

Defendant's Statement: Mr. Clark stated that he was at the Tavern after work on the day of the offense because he wanted to avoid going home because his in-laws were in town for a few days and he dislikes his father-in-law. He said that Mr. Jones instigated the fight by using racial slurs and profanity towards him and throwing the first punch. Mr. Clark stated that he felt his life was threatened by Mr. Jones when he, Mr. Clark, was on the ground and Mr. Jones sat on him. Mr. Clark stated that Mr. Jones was reaching for his neck, and Mr. Clark thought Mr. Jones intended to strangle him. That was why he got his gun and shot him. Mr. Clark stated that he wished he never had gone to the tavern that night. He went on to state that he wishes he had had the "sense to walk out the door rather than fight." But once the fight occurred, he "simply reacted to the threat." Mr. Clark stated that he had legally purchased the gun but did not have a permit to carry a concealed weapon. He explained that he purchased the gun for safety while driving to and from work.

Summary of Court Proceedings: Mr. Clark pled not guilty and claimed self-defense. His case went to trial, which lasted four days, after which a guilty verdict was reached.

Summary of Offender's Background: Mr. Clark does not have any prior arrests. He has been married for five years and he and his wife have a three-year-old son. He has worked at the same trucking company in receiving for the past seven years. He has lived his entire life in Southtown, graduating from high school in 2002. He has 54 college credits earned toward a Bachelor's degree in business.

Assignment 6.7

1. Determine whether legislative acts in your area led to the creation of a community corrections program, as described at the beginning of this section. If your area does not have a community corrections program, research information about such a program in any area in order to answer the following questions:

    a.   How many members are on the board?
    b.   What representation is required to be on the board?
    c.   What type of involvement does the board have in decision making relevant to criminal justice?

2. How many people do you think should be on a community corrections advisory board? Explain your answer.

3. If you were a probation officer in charge of inviting individuals to serve on the community corrections advisory board, what representation do you think would be ideal? Explain your rationale for the choices you made.

4. Using the above example of a case referral to the board and your answer to #3 above, how do you think each person would vote in reference to whether Mr. Clark should be allowed to stay in the community in some type of community corrections program? Explain your answer.

Chapter Seven

Integrating Case Studies with Career Development

Introduction

After having read the case studies, completed a variety of interactive learning activities, and learned about common reports, the reader should now have developed a clearer understanding of employment responsibilities pertaining to the field of corrections. The information may pique the interest of some readers to explore correctional employment opportunities. For others, the information may help solidify their intent to pursue careers in corrections. The information may help other readers decide that corrections is not a job choice for them. If any of these three results occur after reading this book, and hopefully they do, then this book has accomplished the purpose of having readers make informed decisions. To the benefit of everyone—students using this book, the offender population that receives the services provided, and society in general—everyone who chooses work in the field of corrections should enter this employment field informed and knowledgeable about what the job may entail. Negative results are likely to occur if recent graduates of a higher education degree program merely take a job in corrections because they cannot find employment in their chosen field. Job performance and job satisfaction are likely to decrease, turnover is likely to increase, client services are likely to be substandard or marginal, at best, and the reputation of hard-working correctional employees, in general, may be tainted by the actions of persons with no intent of staying in the job.

Yet, it would be a mistake to think that this one book has provided all the information one needs to make important career choices. This book is only one aid among many that can help a student become more informed about employment in the field of corrections. Throughout this chapter, readers will learn about a number of other ways to increase their awareness of what work in corrections is really like. The final chapter of this book also assists the reader in learning about careers in correctional employment in another way by providing responses to questions asked of practitioners in the field about the in's and out's of employment in the broad field of corrections.

Although the information in the following sections is extensive, it is by no means comprehensive. There are many, many means through which one can become informed about employment opportunities and career tracks but what is provided should be enough to give the reader a solid basis from which to start.

Like the previous chapters, each section here is followed by a variety of assignments that are focused on helping the reader become more engaged in the learning process. What makes these assignments slightly different from those in preceding chapters is the need for the readers' personal reflection about careers. The exercises at the end of the chapter require students to integrate what they have learned through the case studies with personal reflection and analysis of career options with the goal of having students recognize whether a career in corrections would be a suitable choice.

Exploring Options

Many college students suffer under the misconception that fulfilling curriculum requirements for their chosen degree will provide them all they need to know to enter their career choice. The instruction they receive will likely increase their knowledge base of specific content and improve their skills and abilities in particular areas relevant to performing well as a student as well as useful in their future jobs. However, unless students intentionally engage in a variety of outside-the-classroom activities, they are likely to have a limited understanding of what the day-to-day responsibilities of various employment opportunities entail.

The following suggestions will assist in filling this awareness gap between in-and-out-of-classroom learning.

Job Shadowing

This strategy has been used for decades. The concept is really quite simple: if you want to know what the job is really like, shadow someone who does that job. Keep in mind that you must spend more than a few hours or even one or two days, to learn the gist of what the job entails. A better idea is to plan on shadowing someone for a whole week long, since people in most professions are likely to have a weekly schedule of activities. Although the day-to-day activities in corrections work are often unpredictable, some structure is usually involved. For example, a probation officer may set up a weekly schedule of office visits on Monday and Wednesday, has Tuesday reserved for court time because that is the day that sentencing occurs, and field visits and writing reports on Thursday and on Friday. Each day the officer is likely to set aside time to complete case notes. Although the officer may have a weekly plan for addressing the job responsibilities, s/he will likely have to make alterations to accommodate situations as they arise, such as going to the jail to talk with a probationer who has been arrested. Spending a week shadowing an officer will provide students a fairly clear idea of what the job, in general, entails.

How does a student arrange to job shadow? The first step is to make contact with agencies that have employees who work the type of job the student is interested in. A college professor or advisor may be able to help direct the student to contacts. In contacting the agency, the student will have to determine if job shadowing is allowable, since some places do not allow students to job shadow, due to liability and confidentiality issues. They will also need to find out what documentation is needed to be allowed to shadow someone for a week. It is important to approach this effort with determination. It may require contacting a number of places to find one that fits the purpose of the student and allows shadowing.

Persistence is a skill that will likely be needed during the job search stage, as well.

Job shadowing can accommodate many students who attend college and work because it does not take the time commitment that internships frequently require. However, if students can participate in an internship, the breadth and depth of learning through experience is probably the preferable means to gain insight into various jobs.

Completing Internships

If students' schedules allow, the best opportunity to learn about jobs is to complete an internship. Colleges have differing requirements, but, in general, internships commonly involve a minimum number of at-site hours and completion of a journal to record what was learned. The number of hours to be completed per credit varies greatly across curriculums; however a number of programs require 40 hours per credit. For example, if a student enrolls in a three-credit-hour internship, s/he will be required to put in 120 hours at the agency of the internship. Spreading this out over a 16-week period, the length of a standard semester, and taking into consideration that students usually do not start their hours the first week of class, the student will spend appropriately eight hours a week involved in the internship. Comparing this to the traditional in-class course, at 3 credit hours, the student will be in the classroom 2.5 hours per week and spend anywhere from 3 to 9 hours per week, on average, in-out-of-class study. In total, this equals 5.5 to 11.5 hours per week or 88 to 184 hours per semester.

Students usually want to know if they are paid while interning. Some internships are paid, but the great majority are not.

An advantage of an internship over job shadowing is that it provides a greater variety of learning experiences and usually offers the student a broader perspective of a job. For example, if a student enrolls in three credit hours of internship with a corrections agency, s/he may have an opportunity to rotate through the various services or divisions provided through the agency, such as legal, administration, case management, and records.

Another advantage of an internship over job shadowing is the increased possibilities for networking, a topic which is discussed in more detail later. Being on site over an extended period of time, the student is much more likely to meet other criminal justice and/or social service employees and learn how the many segments of the system interact one with another. For example, the student interning at a corrections agency may be able to spend one or more days observing budget review hearings by legislators and thus learn more about how decisions that impact corrections services are made while also meeting a variety of people, who function in numerous roles.

Students enrolled in an internship may be required to complete a journal chronicling their learning. Although they may view this as a tedious part of an internship, the journaling, if done well, can increase the development of reflective thinking which, in turn, can help them in making informed decisions about future careers. An example of a student interning in a parole agency illustrates this point. A student reading over the journal entries at the end of the semester may realize that most of the reflections on the job and the people s/he worked with were more negative than positive. This brings up a very important point: it is better that a student realize whether one is well suited to the job before going through the search and hire process than after taking the job and finding out it is not the right job. Such a situation is lose-lose for everyone. The student/new employee is not satisfied, the employer has invested a great deal of time and money in hiring someone who is not going to stay in the job, and the client is likely to receive marginal service.

Perhaps the most significant advantage of appropriate internship placement is the opportunities it affords the student for a future job at the agency. Many students secure employment upon graduation at the agency where they did their internship. Internship supervisors frequently confirm that, all other factors being equal, they often prefer to hire someone who has interned successfully with their agency and whose performance was responsible and professional rather than someone they know little about other than what they see on paper.

So, how do students arrange an internship? The first step is to determine if an internship is a viable option at the college they are attending. If it is, the next step is to determine if the faculty or staff member who oversees internships will assist in locating an internship placement or if students must arrange for the placement themselves. The third step is to meet with the agency where the internship may take place and get answers to questions that may determine whether the time spent in internship at that agency may lead to a positive and valuable experience. What questions should students ask? The following list, although not suitable in every instance, should give students an idea of what type of information is important to gather. Written in the first person, students can use the list below as a starting point in developing their list of questions to have answered.

- Will I be assigned to one person the whole time, or will I work with a variety of people?
- Will I have an opportunity to observe a variety of jobs while interning?
- What work responsibilities will I have as an intern?
- Do I have set hours at the agency each week, or can I vary the times I come in, based on other responsibilities I have?
- Is there an expected dress code?
- Who will complete the paperwork that I need to turn in to the college to earn credit?
- Who should I call if I cannot come in as schedule?
- Is there paperwork I need to complete before starting as an intern?
- Will there be other interns from my college or another college at the agency the same semester I am here?
- Does your agency ever offer an opportunity for paid internships?
- Has your agency hired previous interns?

Answers to the above questions, or ones similar, will help students determine whether or not the agency for the placement is where they want to do the internship. Making this decision, based on an understanding of expectations, is better than taking a placement that is ill-suited to the student's interest and needs.

Volunteer

If a student does not want to job shadow or cannot locate an appropriate contact and the student cannot, for any one of a number of reasons, enroll in an internship, then volunteering hours at an agency is another avenue to pursue. The challenge of this approach to gaining information about jobs is that it seldom involves college resources and depends almost entirely on the students' initiative. Students may not know who to approach or how to initiate the offer to volunteer. Furthermore, not all agencies are well suited to volunteers, as is true for many governmental operations. However, in most cities, many nonprofit organizations function best through the serious efforts and long hours volunteers devote, such as in homeless shelters and food banks. Local civic organizations, the chamber of commerce, large church organizations, the mayor's office, and the college student affairs office are points of contact that can assist students in finding appropriate agencies to volunteer their services and gain job experience.

The advantages of volunteering as a means of learning more about jobs are numerous. The hours are set by the student. How many or how few hours, as well as when to volunteer, is the student's choice. Also, no tuition fees attach to volunteer hours, unless, of course, the hours are part of the requirements of a course. The student can gain varied experiences rather than being restricted to one agency. The student has an opportunity to use volunteer hours at an agency as a trial run to determine if this place is suitable for an internship. It also provides students an opportunity to make contacts that may lead to employment opportunities and also provides students the opportunity of a future reference when applying for jobs. But, aside from other benefits, perhaps, of most personal benefit, is the intrinsic value of volunteering.

Utilize Campus Career Services

Many colleges have a variety of career service resources, including staff that can assist students in the development of resumes and cover letters and provide advice in preparing for job interviews.

This office usually organizes an annual job fair. Other resources include informational packets that provide guides to the steps to follow in searching for employment. The career services office may also have materials available to students on a variety of topics, including test preparation guides for exams commonly used by government agencies and graduate programs, as well as other publications relevant to specific career choices. Staff from career services may also provide presentations in various classes, particularly capstone courses designed for students soon to graduate, and career-development courses included as options in the program curriculum.

Although these services are usually free to students enrolled at the college, the student must take the initiative to access the resources available, such as setting up an appointment to meet with an advisor or simply walking in and asking for assistance. The individual time provided to students is a valuable resource that all students should take advantage of while in school.

Attend Job Fairs

Whether or not students take advantage of meeting with a career services advisor, students should attend as many job fairs as possible. They should attend job fairs sponsored by their own college, by other area colleges, if allowed, and those sponsored by government agencies. Students of any class rank should attend the fairs from freshmen level through their senior year. The more job fairs students attend and the more often they introduce themselves, the more comfortable they will become with the job search process. Students should always present themselves as a professional at job fairs, dressing accordingly. They will likely be given an opportunity to meet representatives from various agencies and, occasionally, be offered an on-site preliminary interview. The networking students establish at a job fair may prove to be a valuable resource as they approach graduation. Students should go to a job fair prepared to ask relevant questions. The following list should assist students with compiling their own list:

- Is your agency currently recruiting for _____?
  Here the student should name a specific position. If the student just asks "Is your agency currently hiring," the answer may be yes but they may be hiring for a position that is totally irrelevant to what the student is looking for in employment.
- Does your agency have internship opportunities in the area of _____?
  Again, it is important to specify the area.
- What does the selection process involve?
- What special skills and abilities are needed for the position in _____?
  Again, name the position.
- May I give you my resume now, or do you prefer that I mail it to your agency?

As is indicated in the last question, it is important for those students who will soon be entering the job search process to take their resume to the job fair. This would not be appropriate for a student to ask who will not be searching for employment for a few years. Whether or not the student can ask questions of the representative at the job fair will depend on whether time is available and whether the agency representative is likely to know the answers. Some agencies send a person from their human resources department; other agencies have a person at the job fair who is currently employed in a specific occupation, such as a police officer or a corrections officer, and yet others have an administrative staff person represent the agency. When students introduce themselves, the representatives are likely to reciprocate and provide information about their positions and their agency. This information should alert students to how detailed their questions can be.

There are many ways to explore career options. It is important to open your mind to various opportunities, try something different, go outside your comfort zone, and talk to many people. The information above names but a few of the ways you can get started to accomplish this. Students could find out about other options through talking with college professors, career services personnel, and other students.

Engaging in Reflection

When developing a career plan, learning about oneself is as important as learning about various career options, searching for a job, and completing the application process. So, what is involved in learning more about yourself? You must engage in reflective thinking or, perhaps a more common term, being insightful. You may wonder how to do this. One of the first steps is to ask yourself, "What does this mean to me?" For example, think back through the cases you read about in chapters two through five. A quick review may remind you of key points. Now ask yourself which of these cases struck a sensitive nerve when you read about the individual represented in the case material. Did you feel repelled, angry, or frustrated? Next, think about why you felt the way you did. Did you feel the person had no basis to act the way s/he did, or did you empathize with the victim but could not understand the offender's behavior? Now, to really explore on a deeper level, try to figure out what triggered those feelings. Is it because you, yourself, have been a victim or personally know someone who has been victimized in a similar way? Maybe you believe strongly in the way things should be and have difficulty understanding anything that goes contrary to that deep-seated belief. Or maybe you have been learning how the criminal justice system ideally should work, but what you learned through the case study has caused you to doubt the veracity of what you have learned. This process requires going beyond the surface explanation why you feel a certain way and digging deeper to understand oneself on a more philosophical level. Not an easy process, this takes practice, as well as time. It is a process that usually cannot be completed in a short time span, with distractions that interfere with focusing your full attention on the major issues. You may have heard the phrase "think it through." Thinking through is the action that is needed for reflection.

On occasions, people depend on the perceptions of others to form opinions and feelings towards particular subjects or situations. In using reflective thinking, the individual gains control for developing opinions and feelings. For example, many students express resistance to the requirement to complete a statistics or re-search class for their major. They may have developed this resistance, based on the opinions expressed by others that statistics is a difficult class that should not be required because it will not be of use in their future careers. Students who accept these opinions of others as true allow external influences to dictate how they feel about the subject. In reflective thinking, students would ask themselves how they feel about taking the class, why they feel that way, and whether the opinions of others are valid.

Applying this concept to career decisions, encourages students to understand better why they decided on the major they did and why they are making the career choice they are making. Such an important life decision should certainly not be dictated by external influences, but should be the result of reflective thinking.

Developing a Degree Plan

Students most likely have already learned that they must complete specific course requirements to complete their degree. They have also probably been informed that they can choose a set number of elective credits. What they may not recognize, however, is that their choice of elective credits may later prove to be very important to their future career options. Looking at the employment search process from the employer's perspective reveals why electives may affect hiring choices.

The number of applicants for an employment opportunity is likely to vary greatly, depending on a number of factors such as national, state, and local economic stability, growth or decrease in government funding, and unemployment rates. The more applicants for a job, the greater the competition for the position and the greater the selection options for the employer. In a competitive job market, the employer can relatively quickly sort through information from the applicant pool and select candidates who stand out as having an edge on the competition. For example, an advertisement for a county juvenile probation officer may include requirements for a Bachelor's degree in social sciences and two years of experience working with juveniles. If the rate of unemployment is high at the time this announcement is released, depending on the location, this one position announcement is likely to elicit hundreds of interested applicants that meet these two basic criteria. In such a case, the employer will screen the applicant information for additional credentials, such as a minor in a foreign language or social work or early childhood development. The employer may select applicants who, as well as meeting the two basic criteria, have also interned in a juvenile probation office or child protective services or participated in a university-sponsored mentoring program.

The point is that students should carefully select what courses they are going to complete to fulfill their elective credits and when they are going to complete these credits. This decision should be based on career planning. To make meaningful elective choices, students need to have an idea of what type of career they plan to pursue upon degree completion. Given that many students begin college without a specific career choice, they should take general education credits early and, if completely unclear on what career path to pursue, take a general introductory course in two or three areas. Delaying elective credits to the junior and senior years will allow students to develop clarity on degree and future career choices. Upperclassmen can better determine their minor or select group course work that will better prepare themselves for future employment.

As another consideration, students may explore the option of completing an independent study under the tutelage of one of their professors. Although independent studies can follow many different tracks, in working with a faculty member, students may be able to use an independent study course to complete, for example, one to six credits of in-depth examination of a particular topic that can open the door for employment opportunities. For example, a student may want to discover whether research has shown that probation supervision, in combination with job development, is more effective in decreasing recidivism than a period of six months in jail during which time the individual participates in a job development program. Knowing the results of the research, and following up with developing a plan to introduce a similar study in the local community, may make a difference in future employment opportunities.

Another important point in developing a degree plan is that, in most cases, the student will need to take the initiative to determine what courses are required to complete a minor. This usually involves going to another department on campus to collect that information. The home department establishes the requirements for the major, but the criteria for requirements relative to minors is controlled by the department offering the minor, not the department of the student's major. The student also is responsible for initiating discussions relevant to the possibility of an independent study project. Employers tend to favor students whose transcripts show evidence of a degree plan that is indicative of individual initiative and creativity. Independent study demonstrates students' self-discipline and ability to complete a major project.

In summary, having a plan for degree completion that positions the student for increased employment opportunities involves much more than merely following the bulletin for degree requirements. It involves the student's participation in individualizing the plan for elective credits specific to future interests.

Increasing Marketability

The suggestions made in previous parts of this chapter could all be considered options to increase your marketability for employment opportunities. However, there are additional options you should consider.

Joining a campus club is one. Many college programs offering criminal justice degrees have established Criminal Justice Student Associations. These groups commonly participate in community service projects, plan topic-related campus events, such as debates between elected officials and town hall meetings, and participate in local and national professional conferences. As well as demonstrating extracurricular involvement, the activities of these clubs often provide students networking opportunities. Inviting practitioners to campus-sponsored events gives students excellent opportunities to introduce themselves to persons who may be involved in a future employment recruitment and selection process. Talking with representatives of agencies at these events provides both parties an opportunity to put a name with a face, which can be beneficial when making later contact for employment purposes. Attending local, state, and national professional conferences gives students another chance to network with other students, as well as faculty from other programs. Participating in community service projects, such as soliciting donations of food and other needed items for the local homeless shelter, provides students an opportunity to network and demonstrate their involvement in extracurricular activities. All of these activities introduce students into the future professional community.

Another suggestion to consider is exploring the possibility of completion of trainings and workshops relevant to specific content areas. For example, a workshop on risk and needs assessment of offender populations may be offered in your area and open to practitioners or college students pursuing social service degrees. Not only would such a workshop provide an opportunity to increase the knowledge base in a particular area but it also offers yet another opportunity for networking with other students and practitioners.

A third way to increase marketability is by serving as a mentor either through a college-sponsored program or through a community agency. Mentoring is not just for adult/youth interactions but also for adults to mentor other adults, such as in job training and adult education programs. Mentoring provides students an opportunity to gain experience by working with offenders and establishing contacts with representatives of various agencies. The experiences gained through mentoring can help students decide if they want to pursue a career in a specific area. Involvement in various court advocacy programs can also provide opportunities for working with various groups with similar learning potential.

In summary, improving marketability entails getting involved in opportunities for learning outside of the traditional classroom setting. This, in turn, expands the potential of establishing a network of contacts that can prove beneficial in future employment searches.

Searching for Employment

The proliferation of Internet capabilities has greatly expanded the possibilities to search for employment. However, the advancements in technology may entail both benefits and challenges. On one hand, searching locally, state-wide, nationally, or even internationally, is now just a click away. This removes the expense and time of getting print copies of newspapers. It also provides an opportunity to search many different sites and to obtain extensive information about the job. However, due to human error, it is subject to limitations. The results of an Internet search depend on the terms used. For example, searching for employment opportunities using the term "counseling programs and offenders" may not produce information about positions under the title "intervention programs for substance abusers." And as strange as it may sound, although the use of technology has spread rapidly, not all agencies post their position openings on the Internet. If they do, they may not use a format that is easy to locate or access.

This potential problem leads to a suggestion about the broad approach necessary when searching for employment. Searching beyond Internet sources may still be useful. Searching newspapers, trade journals, job boards at government buildings and employment offices can also provide valuable information about position announcements.

In addition, a great deal of information about job openings comes through word of mouth. In the previous section the importance of networking was emphasized. The network one establishes with the agencies that have positions sought after is critically important. It is fairly common for people to get a lead on a job opportunity simply by asking persons in the network what they are aware of that is available or will be in the future.

Students seeking employment should also make contact with the agency where they would like to work and set up an appointment to talk with an administrator at the agency. Taking the initiative to do so shows the employer that the student is willing to make the extra effort to seek out positions. It also allows an opportunity for the employer to put a face with a name. Little will be accomplished by calling a general information number for an agency and simply asking if there are currently any employment opportunities. The person answering the phone may not know or may not be interested enough to take the time to advise a random caller asking for such information. For this reason, students should seek out the person who has the most accurate information about agency employment opportunities. This may be the human resources director, a program administrator, or the agency director. Because these people often have very tight schedules, students should ask for a brief period of time, perhaps 15 minutes, and go to the meeting with a list of questions to ask. Students should, of course, start with a brief introduction of their interest area, reason for scheduling the appointment, and brief description of their credentials. The following list of questions can assist students in developing their own specific questions to ask:

- Does your agency currently have any employment opportunities in the area of _____?
- How often does your agency recruit persons for the position of _____ on an annual basis?
- When was the last person hired at your agency for the position of _____?
- Can you advise me of any particular skills or abilities you are seeking in new hires for the position of _____?
- Does your agency now, or in the recent past, have a hiring freeze of any type?
- What promotion opportunities are available for someone in the position of _____?
- What suggestions do you have for a student to prepare for seeking employment in the position of _____ at your agency?
- Where can I locate position announcements for your agency?
- Is there an online application process, or do applicants complete a paper form?

One last point in reference to employment searches: follow-up is very important. Whether by phone, letter, or an email, to the employer's human resources department, follow-up is often necessary to determine the status of the search. It also indicates to the agency that the applicant is still interested in the job and is taking the initiative to determine if the position has been filled. Applicants should inquire as to how long their applications will be kept on file for future position openings. Making follow-up contact with the agency also provides applicants an avenue to inquire whether they need to provide any additional information to assist in the screening process.

Preparing for the Selection Process

Applicants need to be aware of the employer's selection process. Being aware of the methods will assist the applicant in anticipating the type of information that may be needed at various stages in the process as well as approximately how long the selection process will take. Employment offers in criminal justice employment in the government sector are seldom quickly made. It is not unheard of for the selection process to take a year or more to complete. Being aware of all of the steps involved and the length of time to complete the process will help the applicant decide whether to apply for multiple jobs at one time rather than waiting for a final decision on one job before completing applications for others. The selection process is often somewhat quicker in the private sector because fewer steps are required to complete the process.

What methods or strategies do employers use to determine which applicant to select for the position? Although it depends on the job and the agency, some common ones are interviews, tests (such as reading comprehensive and writing), personality inventories, psychological evaluations, and scenarios. Although polygraph testing continues to be used by some agencies, this method has decreased in popularity in recent years. Depending on the position requirements, physical agility testing may also be used. Background checks may also be a part of the screening process, as well as the requirement of educational, personal, and/or employment references. In government employment, the background check is frequently the most time-intensive part of the screening process. How thorough the check is depends on the security level required for the employment position.

Most of these methods are self explanatory, but some details may not be obvious. For example, the interviewing process may entail one or more steps and more than one person. In fact, many agencies use group or panel interviews. If applicants are not aware that this is part of the process, they may feel somewhat overwhelmed when entering the interview room with nine people around the table if they were expecting one. Therefore, applicants should ascertain information about the interview process prior to showing up at the scheduled time. In regard to the questions to be answered at an interview, there is great variation. Questions may probe the applicant's educational qualifications and prior work experience, but because this information is usually readily available on a resume or application form, many employers have found it more beneficial to use interview time to pose questions based on scenarios. These generally involve describing a complex work situation and asking the applicant to analyze the situation and propose a solution.

In regard to testing, an agency may use a content based test to determine knowledge levels pertinent to the job. For example, a state probation and parole department may use a test that includes questions on legal issues, court processes, and supervision requirements. The test may include multiple choice, true/false, and/or short essay. If an applicant finds out that part of the process is to pass a test, an applicant should find out as much as possible about the likely content of the test and determine if there is any way that s/he can better prepare to do well.

In contrast to knowledge, skills, and abilities tests, an applicant cannot prepare for a personality inventory or psychological evaluation. The best advice is for the applicant to answer honestly since most inventories and evaluation procedures have built-in means to determine if the applicant is falsifying responses.

The main point to take away from the information in this section is that the more applicants know about the selection process, the better prepared they can be to make informed decisions.

Summary

There are many ways to engage in career development. This chapter focused on six ways for students to improve their chances of working in a career that will result in high job satisfaction and job performance.

1. Exploring options
2. Engaging in reflection
3. Developing a degree plan
4. Improving marketability
5. Searching for employment
6. Preparing for the selection process

The assignments below are intended to assist students to develop their own personal career plan.

Assignment 7.1

1. Chapters 2 through 5 of this book focused on case studies in corrections. If you were to pursue correctional employment, what particular area (institutional, community, working with juveniles or adults, etc.) do you feel you would be best suited for? Explain how your answer was based on reflective thinking, being detailed about what about you, personally, would be best suited for a particular career track.

2. Of the offenders depicted in the cases provided in chapters 2 through 5, which three do you think you would have the most difficult time providing service? Explain your answer, detailing what about these particular cases would be difficult for you and why.

3. If you were to conduct an independent study focused on topics in corrections, what would be the topic? Which professors in your program do you think might be willing to supervise the independent study? What do you think would be the required work product to receive the number of credits you would enroll in for an independent study?

4. Having read the cases in chapters 2 through 5 and reviewed the reports contained in Chapter 6, what college minor do you think would be of most benefit in obtaining correctional employment? Explain your answer, providing relevant information from the chapter(s). Does your college offer such a minor? If so, what are the requirements? If not, what course grouping (15 credits) do you think would provide you the type of learning that would be beneficial in obtaining correctional employment?

5. Determine what mentoring opportunities are available in your area. What are the requirements for serving as a mentor? If you were required to participate as a mentor as part of your degree program, what mentoring opportunity would you choose?

6. Determine what professional organization(s) related to corrections has a meeting in the coming year. Where will the meeting be held? What opportunities are available for college students to participate in the meetings?

7. Make a list of five websites pertaining to correctional employment opportunities. Search those sites and make a list of five correctional employment opportunities currently being advertised. In gathering this information, make sure to note the particulars about each job such as educational and experience requirements and any particular knowledge, skills, or abilities needed. Do you think you would presently or will upon graduation meet the requirements for application? Explain why or why not. What deficiencies do you have, if any?

8. Based on the list of five correctional employment opportunities you found, determine the screening methods involved in three separate position announcements.

9. Make a list of questions that you, as the job applicant, would like to ask at the job interview. Get into a group of 3 or 4 other people and share your list. Develop one master list of five questions your group thinks would be most important and appropriate to ask at a job interview.

Chapter Eight

Practitioner Interviews

Interviews

In exploring career choices in corrections, the applicant should evaluate the differences in employers and work settings of government or private employment and community or institutional work. Additionally, prospective employees can frequently choose employment focused on working with adults or children and, sometimes, working with males or females exclusively. For example, if applicants seek employment at a correctional facility, they need to consider whether they want to work with juveniles or adults and whether they want to work with males or females. Of course, in community corrections, such as probation and parole, working with only one gender is not commonly an option. However, the vast majority of the offender population is male.

Another consideration is specific job responsibilities as depicted in the job description, which also includes the education and experience requirements for the position. The following list of career options in corrections is by no means meant to be exhaustive but, instead, is provided to give the reader an idea of the variability available if considering a career in this field:

- Probation/Parole Officer
- Correctional Counselor
- Case Manager
- Correctional Officer
- Correctional Administrator
- Social Worker
- Classification Officer

- Training Personnel
- Legal Advisor
- Court Appointed Site Monitor
- Accreditation Reviewer
- Budgetary Analyst
- Correctional Recreation Specialist
- Educator
- Vocational facilitator
- Psychologist

Although job descriptions are compiled to specify clearly the responsibilities of the position, they are often limited in providing the type of information that is useful to a person trying to decide whether the job is an appropriate career option to pursue. As mentioned in the previous chapter, one way to obtain information that can be helpful in deciding among career choices is to interview persons currently in the positions being considered.

Following is a brief questionnaire that this author developed to obtain responses from a variety of persons currently employed in corrections. The next sections provide the questions asked, a summary of the process used for inviting participation, the responses given, a summary of the key points from the responses, and closing comments.

The Questionnaire

1. What is the position title of your current employment with the Department of Correction?
2. How long have you been employed with the Department of Correction?
3. How long have you been in your current position?
4. What type of education and/or work experience is required for the position?
5. What are the average working hours?
6. Are there opportunities for advancement? If so, to what position title? How many years, on average, are needed prior to being eligible for advancement?

7. What special skills are required for the position in which you are currently employed such as computer skills, public speaking skills, etc.?
8. How frequently do job opportunities become available in the position you are currently employed?
9. What primary job responsibilities do you perform on a daily basis?
10. What made you decide to pursue employment in criminal justice?
11. Does this position require overtime and, if so, what is the average number of hours per week or month?
12. Is it possible to flex your work schedule in order for you to attend continuing education?
13. What are the things you like best about your job?
14. If there was one thing you could change about your job, what would it be?

Participant Invitation

Contact was made with representatives of adult and juvenile corrections facilities and probation and parole services. An email invitation was sent inviting them to voluntarily respond to a questionnaire containing the above listed fourteen questions. Respondents were asked to provide their answers either through email communication or regular mail. They were assured that their responses would be confidential with no clear identifiers reported. They were also informed of the purpose of asking for their involvement. As stated in the invitation, the purpose of gathering their feedback is to provide students with information about what it is really like working in a variety of correctional positions. Students all too often base career decisions on faulty information, mainly from popular media sources, just to later learn that the job is nothing like what they imagined it to be. An obvious conclusion is that the more informed a person is in making employment choices, the greater the likelihood that job satisfaction and job performance will increase and job turnover will decrease.

Employment Positions of Respondents and Length of Employment

The length of time in corrections employment of the respondents in the following positions ranged from 4 to 30+ years. The majority of the respondents have been employed in corrections for a decade or more and have held their current position for approximately 2 to 20+ years.

- Correctional Lieutenant
- Correctional Sergeant
- Manager — Probation Department
- Adult Probation Officer
- Youth Service Supervisor
- Psychiatric Social Service Specialist
- District Supervisor
- Juvenile Program Director
- Superintendent
- Senior Parole Agent/Trainer

Responses to General Questions

Instead of providing responses to questions 4 through 12 on an individual basis, the following information represents each response per position of respondent grouped by question. Responses to question 13 and 14 are provided in summary form, without identification of the position the respondent holds, due to the personal nature of the questions. In most cases, the responses are given verbatim. However, some responses were paraphrased in order to eliminate personal identifiers.

Q#4: What type of education or work experience is required for the position?

Correctional Lieutenant: A formal education is good to have, but 1–3 years of supervisor experience and knowledge of policy and procedures is all that is required.

Correctional Sergeant: Two years of full-time custody experience in a correctional institution along with a high school diploma or possession of a General Educational Development (GED) certificate; must have successfully completed the Correctional Training Institute Program or a similar training program acceptable to the Department of Correction; accredited college training may substitute for the required experience with a maximum substitution of 2 years; law enforcement or military law enforcement experience may substitute for the required experience with a maximum substitution of 1 year.

Manager—Probation Department: A Bachelor's degree from an accredited institution; hands-on experience working in a corrections or social service field.

Probation Officer: A Bachelor's degree from an accredited college and completion of the certification test and Probation Officer Orientation within six months of being hired; completion of 12 hours of continuing education hours a year to remain current as a certified Probation Officer; it was very helpful that I volunteered for a period of time with court services as I was able to learn on-the-job duties as well as meet people within the Department and get my name recognized once a position opened up; I have found that if you are familiar with the organization, through internship or volunteering, you are more likely to be selected not only for an interview but for the job.

Youth Service Supervisor: 5 years correctional officer experience.

Psychiatric Social Service Specialist: BA in a related field.

District Supervisor:	Bachelor's Degree plus 2 years minimum experience in corrections/law enforcement.
Program Director:	Bachelors degree, 4 years full time paid clinical experience, 2 years full time paid supervisory experience.
Superintendent:	Bachelors degree and 3 years of correctional management.
Senior Parole Agent/ Trainer:	Five years full-time professional experience in correctional counseling, criminology, parole/probation work, law enforcement, social work, or a related area; five years of full-time experience in protective services may substitute for the required experience only. Accredited college training may substitute for the required experience on a year for year basis; must successfully complete the Correctional Training Academy and all required training prior to granting permanent status.

Q#5: *What are the average working hours?*

Correctional Lieutenant:	8–12 hours per day
Correctional Sergeant:	12 hour shifts based on a 3 and 4 day alternating work week
Manager — Probation Department:	40–45 hours a week
Probation Officer:	40 hours per week; overtime is not allowed but compensatory time in the maximum amount of 72 hours is allowable.
Youth Service Supervisor:	7.5 hours per day
Psychiatric Social Service Specialist:	8.5 hours per day
District Supervisor:	45 hours per week
Program Director:	40+ per week
Superintendent:	55 hours per week

Senior Parole Agent/ Trainer:	37.5 hours per week

Q#6: Are there opportunities for advancement? If so, to what position title? How many years, on average, are needed prior to being eligible for advancement?

Correctional Lieutenant:	Correctional Captain; at least 1–3 years supervisor experience within the department.
Correctional Sergeant:	Yes, there are; if in custody the next advancement would be to the rank of Correctional Lieutenant; Three years of full-time custody experience in a correctional institution plus one year full-time experience as a correctional supervisor.
Manager—Probation Department:	I was informed when I began employment as a Probation Officer that opportunities for advancement were extremely limited. However, with a little initiative, positive attitude, willingness to put in extra work, show some leadership abilities, being in the right place at the right time and perhaps an intangible as getting along with other management personnel, a management position may be available. There are three different management positions allowed in the probation system: a supervisory Probation Officer position, Assistant Chief Probation Officer and Chief Probation Officer. At least three years experience in a Probation Officer position would be a good starting point before assuming a management position.
Probation Officer:	Within the Department there is little opportunity for advancement. There are a total of six supervisory positions. On the adult side, there is the Director, Chief Probation Officer, Assistant Probation Officer, and Manager of the Probation Office. On the juvenile side, there is a Chief Probation Officer and an Assistant Chief Probation Officer. To my knowledge, once an opening occurs, any current officer is eligible to apply. For all probation officers, compensation

is increased with years of service as well as further education obtained. These monetary amounts are set by the State. Extra compensation is provided to those officers handling the supervision of volunteers/internships as well as the sex-offender caseloads.

Youth Service Supervisor:	One level for advancement; Commander; 5 years.
Psychiatric Social Service Supervisor:	Many opportunities for advancement ... from supervisor to superintendent; needed years are different for each advancement.
District Supervisor:	Very little. Only 9 District Supervisors in the State. Above myself in Parole is an Assistant Director and the Director.
Program Director:	Yes, there are a myriad of opportunities across all agencies. Each particular opportunity would be determined by the position being vacated or created. Eligibility would be determined by job qualifications and years of state service.
Superintendent:	Director of a Division of the DOC, such as Regional Director of Operations.
Senior Parole Agent/ Trainer:	District Supervisor (Supervisor 5): Seven years full-time professional experience in correctional counseling, criminology, parole or probation work, law enforcement, social work or related required; plus one year full-time administrative, managerial, or supervisory experience in any of the above areas.

Q#7: What special skills are required for the position in which you are currently employed such as computer skills, public speaking skills, etc.?

Correctional Lieutenant:	Knowledge of policy and procedure, good communication skills, at least some formal training in computers.
Correctional Sergeant:	Basic computer skills are needed. Provide direct supervision over correctional officers which may include hiring, interviewing, approval of leave requests and performance reviews.

Manager — Probation Department:	Good communication skills are a priority. This would include good writing skills such as grammar, punctuation and spelling. Although this sounds trite but in a Court setting where good writing skills are mandatory, this is how you communicate with the Court, the Prosecuting Attorney and defense lawyer with different types of Court reports. Probably the biggest change that I have seen in the job duties and functions of a Probation Officer and other Court officials, is the use of computers to gather and disseminate information. Good keyboarding skills are very helpful in the preparation of Court reports, letters and email correspondence. Verbal communication skills are important in dealing with the volume of people on probation and being able to process information received from them. This would include applying techniques such as Motivational Interviewing, risk assessments, and knowledge of community resources to assist the individual on probation to fulfill their Court orders and lead a law-abiding lifestyle. Time management skills are important in being able to manage a high caseload with a large volume of telephone calls, e-mail requests and last minute rush jobs.
Probation Officer:	The requirements for a Probation Officer position were stated above in question number four. However, skills that are extremely helpful in this position are as follows: the ability to speak publicly, the ability to remain objective and separate personal feelings from job duties, excellent writing skills, knowledge of the criminal justice system, and the ability to work under the pressure of deadlines. Being a Probation Officer requires you to testify in Court and meet with convicted or adjudicated people; introverted people struggle with the ability to speak with clients, and in open Court regarding their case management of these people. The Courts are continuously ordering reports with deadlines. Clear, concise, and coherent reports need to be prepared. Time management skills are help-

ful, as caseloads can blossom into 400 clients. So as you meet with your 400 clients, you are expected to know each of their cases, prepare reports when directed to do so, be able to testify in Court as requested to do so and network with community providers to ensure all 400 clients' Court orders are being fulfilled and notify the Court if those terms are not being fulfilled. Sometimes the details provided regarding the crimes can create personal biases, so you have to separate yourself from your personal feelings, be objective and monitor that the client is completing Court orders.

Youth Service Supervisor: Public speaking and communication skills.

Psychiatric Social Service Specialist: Communication, computer skills, psychiatric and sociology background; public speaking; counseling; etc.

District Supervisor: Public relations skills are a must as I am working with 12 counties. Computer skills also a must as we work with many different applications and law enforcement programs. Must also be familiar with department fiscal and personnel policy.

Program Director: Clinical, crisis management, stress management, interpersonal, supervisory, organizational, verbal, written, public speaking, mediation/conflict management, customer service, analytical, etc.

Superintendent: All of the above (computer skills, public speaking skills) including basic understanding of DOC policy/operational practices; budgeting/procurement; leadership and management; supervision/ organizational theory; correctional theory; anything in the social sciences; basic understanding of personnel rules, employee evaluations and associated labor laws, etc.; basic understanding how state government operates; legislative/political issues; media relations; basic understanding of the state correctional code; problem resolution.

Senior Parole Agent/ Trainer:	As a parole agent public speaking, effective communication skills, criminal justice and court system overview, observation skills, and field safety are very important special skills.

Q#8: How frequently do job opportunities become available in the position you are currently employed?

Correctional Lieutenant:	Not so frequently; maybe every 5 years.
Correctional Sergeant:	It varies unlike correctional officers; there are only a certain amount of Sergeant positions within the facility.
Manager — Probation Department:	Due to the local economy, Probation Officer openings have decreased remarkably. Staff are staying in their positions for a much longer period of time and turnover is less. However, looking to the future, a number of Probation Officers should be retiring in the next 5–10 years which would lead to position openings. However, you can not accurately predict how technology will impact the local, state and national economy and job functions may change over the next decade. It is important to be flexible and keep the doors open for job possibilities in the future.
Probation Officer:	I believe job opportunities within the Department seldom become available because the Commissioners have only granted the Department a certain amount of positions. A position will open up when both an Officer leaves and the Commissioners approve our Department's request to fulfill that position or the Commissioners approve adding more positions within the Department.
Youth Service Supervisor:	Not many.
Psychiatric Social Service Specialist:	Every couple years.
District Supervisor:	Rare. There have been 3 supervisors at this District in the past 30 years.
Program Director:	Rarely.

Superintendent:	Probably 2–3 positions open per year.
Senior Parole Agent/ Trainer:	Job opportunities in parole services are very slim as there is very little turnover compared to the rest of the Department of Corrections. Because of the little turnover parole services job opportunities are very competitive.

Q#9: What primary job responsibilities do you perform on a daily basis?

Correctional Lieutenant:	Assign on duty staff to emergency teams, complete and review reports, and ensure accountability for approximately 3300 offenders and about 200 staff.
Correctional Sergeant:	Maintaining the safety and security of the facility I work in by making sure offenders and staff are following the policies.
Manager — Probation Department:	Review and proofread Court reports completed by Probation Officers to be filed with the Court. Complete casework as needed on my own caseload. Assist in maintaining casework as required when staff is on leave and other absences. Review and assist Probation Officers Court dockets and orders received from the different Courts. Perform drug tests on probationers as needed. Discuss with other Administrative staff Court procedures, staff issues and case management problems.
Probation Officer:	I meet with the clients on my caseload in my office. I review the client's court orders for their term of probation. I follow up with local community providers, such as addictions treatment providers, to make sure that my clients are in compliance with Court ordered treatment. I administer drug screens. I prepare reports as needed to inform the Courts of my clients' progress while completing their Terms of Probation. I would say that my duties are 50% meeting with people, 25% paperwork and 25%

networking with community providers. I make sure my caseload completes their terms of probation and I notify the Court if they do not complete those terms or Court orders.

Youth Service Specialist: Performance base standard and training.

Psychiatric Social Service Specialist: I complete any and all tasks for the juveniles I am responsible. These tasks vary due to my population.

District Supervisor: Daily, perform all administrative functions related to budget planning, personnel issues, supervision of staff, and office maintenance in accordance with Department of Correction directions. Pass a yearly audit identifying compliance with budgetary guidelines and that staff appraisals are completed within time frames. Daily, monitor, evaluate and interact with Parole Agents ensuring that they continue to meet the standards and principles of professional case management. Determine that techniques used by staff during offender intervention promote the Department's mission. During the Supervisors performance review, the District Supervisor justifies their degree of interaction with Parole staff to meet the performance expectation. Continually meet with agencies, association, and public officials, to develop partnerships in supporting the Department's Mission to provide a positive and supportive environment for offender re-integration into the community. During the Supervisors performance review, the District Supervisor justifies their degree of interaction with community resources in order to meet the performance expectation. The District Supervisor semi-annually upgrades the Parole Roster of community support groups. Continually develop short term goals and long range plans for improving Parole functions while understanding the importance of achieving results, goals, and objectives within required time frames. Demonstrate an ability to establish priorities and work sequences in coordinating staff efforts, maintaining work flow, and meeting deadlines. Maintain a report card of short and long term goals completed with monthly progress report. Provide support in maintaining the standards of professional case management during periods of time when staff are absent, terminate employment with the state or retire. Participate in offender probation cause and team management hearings and offender program staffing. During Supervisors performance review, the District Supervisor justifies their degree of interaction in order to meet the performance expectation.

Program Director:

Supervisory: Supervise counselors and other departments as assigned, evaluation/performance appraisals, interviews/hiring, training, etc.
Clinical: Intake interview and parent calls, individual group and family counseling, program development, implementation, and evaluation, documentation, etc.
Administrative: Reports, committees, tours, meetings, surveys, phone calls and messages, audits, etc.
Other duties as assigned: Supervise interns, public speaking, facility tours, inter-departmental training

Superintendent:

Daily briefings on all operations/programs/ problem issues and community based issues; holding staff and offenders accountable; daily awareness of offender population, including touring the facility, talking to staff and offenders, understanding the tone of the facility; daily inspections; employee supervision, setting the goals of the facility and following up on adherence/problems with achieving these short term and long term goals/initiatives and tasks expenditures and procurement and managing the budget; interfacing with the demands of Central Administration; reading literature, research and policy; completing reports, memo's, e-mails, returning telephone calls and reading

mail from internal as well as external inquiries;
preparation for coming initiatives, daily problem solving with all aspects of the facility operation; approving employee leave time, staffing
on shifts, handling routine personnel matters
related to sick leave, disability, employee com-
mendation/discipline.

Senior Parole Agent/
Trainer:

Senior Parole Agent maintains a caseload of
parolees, providing services aimed at successful transition of offenders into the community.
Serves in an assigned geographical area. Con-
ducts duties with limited supervision, reporting directly to a Parole Officer's Supervisor.
Incumbent must possess thorough knowledge
of laws, rules, department policy and procedure concerning the supervision of paroled offenders. Incumbent performs the vast majority
of the duties independently in the field. Incumbent serves as department representative
in the community at large working with local
officials, law enforcement, schools, employers
and families. Contacts are with a wide variety
of people and are typically made alone. Final reports are usually reviewed with supervisor for
basic content. Supervisor must rely on the incumbent's decisions regarding parole violators.
Missing information from community investigations could jeopardize the safety of the public.

Q#10: *What made you decide to pursue employment in criminal justice?*

Correctional Lieutenant: Father was a police officer and I wanted to follow in his foot steps.

Correctional Sergeant: When trying to figure out what I would want
to do I looked at a career that would always be
in a demand for jobs. Since there will always
be crime I figured a career in criminal justice
would be the best choice.

Manager—Probation Department:	The job description of a Probation Officer was a position that I felt with my employment history, education and job skills, would be a good fit for my career.
Probation Officer:	I took an elective class that sounded interesting. It fit into my schedule. I was hooked then. I have discovered that I operate in an all or nothing type of mentality and thrive on rules. Criminal statutes fascinated me. The criminal justice system fascinated me. I really think I would eventually like to become a lawyer someday. I love how I can make arguments in Court.
Youth Service Supervisor:	Like working with juveniles.
Psychiatric Social Service Specialist:	I like the population.
District Supervisor:	Degree in Forensic Science from college.
Program Director:	The road less traveled.
Superintendent:	Interested in the social services.
Senior Parole Agent/Trainer:	I was employed with the Department of Correction after graduating from college. I was hired in the Department as an officer working on housing units at a facility. As I promoted up through the ranks in the Department I found my resting place with parole services. I enjoy my current position with parole services as it provides new challenges that make me think outside of the box and places me directly in the community working with the public and local law enforcement agencies which is why I pursued a job in criminal justice.

Q#11: Does this position require overtime and, if so, what is the average number of hours per week or month?

| Correctional Lieutenant: | No, unless you are a member of one of 24 hr on call emergency teams or you are dealing with |

some type of emergency (ex: completing reports).

Correctional Sergeant: Overtime is not required.

Manager — Probation   The position requires overtime when necessary
Department: to complete assigned job duties. The caseloads
                       are so large and the Court's and state Judicial
                       Center's expectations differ from the realities
                       "on the ground" so that prioritizing your case-
                       load and time management skills are required.
                       Some management positions require 50–60+
                       hour work weeks to complete minimal demands
                       during staff leaves as there are no other options
                       available to complete the assigned caseload.

Probation Officer: Our Department is not authorized for over-
                       time. We are allowed to accrue compensatory
                       time. It is accumulated on the honor system,
                       as we keep track of those hours ourselves. How-
                       ever we are only allowed to accrue 72 hours in
                       compensatory time. It is at the individual Of-
                       ficer's discretion to accrue this time. The ex-
                       pectation is that you "get your work done."

Youth Service Supervisor: No.

Psychiatric Social Service No.
Specialist:

District Supervisor: We are not paid overtime. Extra hours occur
                       regularly as issues arise. There is no specific av-
                       erage per say. I can work 45–50 one week and
                       40 the next.

Program Director: Yes, 20–30 hours.

Superintendent: Schedule is not entirely fixed and hours of work
                       are dependent on facility needs, events, prob-
                       lems, etc. Superintendent is on call 24/7 with
                       a blackberry/cell phone for inquiries/response.
                       Generally the job entails 50–60 hours weekly,
                       some weeks less and some more, depending on
                       the demands of the week. Evening and week-
                       end hours for events and emergencies are some-

times necessary. This time can decrease to the extent that the superintendent has good mid-level management and supervision to foresee problems and handle.

Senior Parole Agent/ Trainer:

This position can require overtime on an emergency basis for major altercations.

Q#12: Is it possible to flex your work schedule in order for you to attend continuing education?

Correctional Lieutenant:

Yes, with the permission of our Custody Supervisor (Major).

Correctional Sergeant:

Yes, the Department of Correction concerning correctional staff will provide a flex schedule so that education can be continued.

Manager — Probation Department:

Staff are allowed to flex their work hours with limitations depending on the amount of hours flexed to attend continuing education, the ability of the person to work on their own and the nature of their specific job function.

Probation Officer:

Yes and no. Each person's circumstances are different and would need to be addressed with their particular supervisor, as the overall Department does not object to obtaining higher education.

Youth Service Supervisor: Yes it can with the approval of the facility head.

Psychiatric Social Service Specialist:

Yes.

District Supervisor:

This is permissible with Director approval.

Program Director:

This job requires the incumbent to be here at least between the hours of 6:00 a.m. and 6:00 p.m., my normal work hours being 8:00 a.m.–4:00 p.m.

Superintendent:

Yes.

Senior Parole Agent/   Yes.
Trainer:

The responses to questions 13 and 14 are summarized without identification through specific employment position due to the personal nature of the questions.

Q#13: *What are the things you like best about your job?*

the camaraderie with colleagues
being able to be a role model for staff and offenders
having a positive effect on someone's life
working in a Court environment
the challenges of the job
involves people from all walks of life
love the people I work with
meeting new people
preparing reports
teaching staff
personal interactions with juveniles
being in the community, working with the numerous service providers
    in law enforcement, substance abuse treatment, mental health
    treatment, community corrections, etc.
working with kids and their families
working with my co-workers
the opportunity to enhance their quality of life
short term and long term challenges
each day is extremely varied
managing facility goals and problems to successful resolution
experiencing success with offender transitioning to release
the size of caseloads that are assigned

Q#14: *If there was one thing you could change about your job, what would it be?*

better pay for staff
more staff
better relations with government officials
politics—it is the little things that are politically controlled that I
    don't enjoy
to have a published training plan completed before our training plan
    is due
more field work with my agents

in a perfect world, more operating capital; in the real world, nothing

more time to devote to long term projects/goals; daily demands, which are an important part of the job, continually take away time from managing the goals and initiatives of the facility

the size of caseloads

Summary of Key Points

A number of common themes emerge from the information provided through the questionnaire responses. First, regardless of position, it is apparent that there is commonality in the skills required for completing the responsibility of the job: computer skills, excellent communication skills (written and verbal), and time management skills. The emphasis placed on the need for excellent writing skills, as well as the ability to communicate with a wide variety of stakeholders is apparent. Second, many of the respondents indicated the wide variability in the duties of their employment position. Third, the opportunities for employment in supervisory and management positions in corrections appear to be somewhat limited. This may, in part, be due to the instability of the national economy which tends to encourage people to stay in their current employment. It may also be due to the longevity of employment of many of the respondents; people have a tendency to stay in their correctional employment. As reflected in the list of responses to the question, *What are the things you like best about your job?* people appear to find a great deal of intrinsic satisfaction with their employment. The more satisfied employees are with what they are doing, the more likely it is that they will stay. Fewer positions will be open if turnover is decreased. Fourth, although the responses indicated, in general, the importance of completing reports the responses also pointed out the importance of being a "people person." Last, although many of the respondents indicated that they work more than 40 hours per week, when asked, *If there was one thing you could change about your job, what would it be?* none of the respondents indicated that they wished they did not have to work long hours, another indication that, in general, they like what they are doing.

Closing Comments

The material covered in this chapter points to the importance of being informed about what each correctional job entails, directly from the source, the practitioner. Students are commonly told by their professors that writing and public speaking skills are very important. Perhaps what has been missing in making this point is the link to future careers. The advantage that today's students have over those who have a lengthy history of employment in corrections is that the great majority of students have already developed many of the computer skills that are critical to the successful completion of employment responsibilities. In combination, communication and computer skills appear to be key elements to most, if not all, the employment positions for which responses were obtained. But the responses also indicate the need to use these skills in combination with a desire to work with people to achieve successful outcomes. Therefore, students are well advised to reflect on whether they feel comfortable in working with offenders and other criminal justice professionals and the public at large. In combination, the information portrayed in the case studies and gained from completion of chapter assignments, all point to the importance of combining all of these skills and abilities with content knowledge to achieve positive results.

Index

Accreditation, 65, 78, 82, 83, 138

Aftercare, 47, 61–63

Budget(s), 66–69, 73, 81, 83, 121, 146, 149, 150

Caseload(s), 34, 63, 65, 69–72, 86, 99, 103, 144, 145, 148, 151, 153, 155, 156

Case Management Plan(s), 9, 10, 13, 14, 17, 31, 34, 37, 43, 58

Case notes, 60, 97, 101–110, 119

Child abuse, 21, 23, 24, 43, 64

Child neglect, 21, 23, 24, 43, 50, 52, 54, 56, 64

Child Protective Services, 22, 43, 50, 54, 62, 128

Community corrections advisory board, 113, 116 referrals, 85, 113, 114

Community service, 25, 46, 70, 90, 129, 130

Day Treatment, 11, 29, 38–41

Drug Court, 14, 29, 44–46, 88, 90

Drug use, 16, 25, 26, 32, 39, 41, 45, 55

Electronic monitoring, 14, 29, 34, 36

Family Intervention, 47, 50, 52

First Offender Program, 47–49

Good time, 8, 17, 35, 72, 101, 112

Group counseling, 25, 45, 46, 52, 53, 60, 95, 97, 101, 106, 107, 109, 150

Halfway House, 7, 14–17

House Arrest, 29, 41, 42

Human resources management, 65, 76, 78

Inhalant abuse, 53, 55

Inmate programs, 65, 72–74

Mental Health court, 22–24 developmental delays, 39, 63 facility, 21 intellectual disability, 11, 22, 62

IQ, 11, 22, 38, 62

major depression, 33

paranoid schizophrenia, 11, 22

personality disorder, 11, 18, 33

psychotropic medications, 22

Parole Plan, 32–34, 85, 110–113

Parole violation, 85, 99, 100

revocation, 92, 99, 102

Plea Agreement, 8, 15, 24, 30, 38

Presentencing Report(s), 8, 9, 11, 38, 41, 42, 62, 69, 70, 85, 86, 93, 94, 96, 97, 114

Probation violation, 40, 43, 70, 85, 91, 93, 94–100, 104, 108, 110

Psychological evaluation, 9, 10, 18, 21, 33, 38, 114, 133, 134

Receiving and Diagnostic Center, 18

Re-entry, 73, 74

Re-integration, 149

Risk and Needs Assessment, 9, 31, 105, 130

Semi-independent living, 13, 62, 63

Sex offenders, 59–61, 70

Substance abuse, 5, 7, 16, 24, 47, 53, 54, 74, 95, 101, 106, 131, 155

Suicide, 33

Vocational Program, 33, 74, 92

Work Release, 7, 17, 19, 20